MORGAN KNOWLES

THE VISIBILITY METHOD

How To Cope With Anxiety For Women

The VISIBILITY Method
on
How to Cope with Anxiety

How to Deal with Anxiety and Depression –
Cognitive Behavioral Therapy (CBT) for
Anxiety in Women

Morgan Knowles

Table of Contents

Introduction .... Page 3

Chapter 1: Visualization - How You Start to Use Cognitive Behavioral Therapy Every Day .... Page 12

Chapter 2: Intention - Turning Your Anxiety Into A Routine .... Page 27

Chapter 3: Switch - How You Pinpoint and Change Harmful Thoughts Page 40

Chapter 4: Invalidate - How You Eradicate and Rebuild Your Core Beliefs .... Page 60

Chapter 5: Basic Enlightenment - How You Stay in the Present .... Page 72

Chapter 6: Idling - How You Move Forward and Just Get Started .... Page 85

Chapter 7: Let Go - How You Really Let Go and Remove Worry and Fear from Your Mind .... Page 97

Chapter 8: Instruct - How You Tell Your Mind to Release the Pent Up Anger Inside You .... Page 106

Chapter 9: Time - It's Not Going to Change Overnight .... Page 114

Chapter 10: Yourself - Tomorrow is a New Day .... Page 124

Conclusion .... Page 133

© Copyright Morgan Knowles 2021 - All rights reserved.

The content contained within this book may not be reproduced, duplicated or transmitted without direct written permission from the author or the publisher.

Under no circumstances will any blame or legal responsibility be held against the publisher, or author, for any damages, reparation, or monetary loss due to the information contained within this book. Either directly or indirectly. You are responsible for your own choices, actions, and results.

Legal Notice:

This book is copyright protected. This book is only for personal use. You cannot amend, distribute, sell, use, quote or paraphrase any part, or the content within this book, without the consent of the author or publisher.

Disclaimer Notice:

Please note the information contained within this document is for educational and entertainment purposes only. All effort has been executed to present accurate, up to date, and reliable, complete information. No warranties of any kind are declared or implied. Readers acknowledge that the author is not engaging in the rendering of legal, financial, medical or professional advice. The content within this book has been derived from various sources. Please consult a licensed professional before attempting any techniques outlined in this book.

By reading this document, the reader agrees that under no circumstances is the author responsible for any losses, direct or indirect, which are incurred as a result of the use of the information contained within this document, including, but not limited to, — errors, omissions, or inaccuracies.

Just for you

A FREE GIFT TO OUR READERS

Get The Top 7 Ways To Help Manage Anxiety - You can start using these top tips right away, which will help you to control the most aggressive mood swings and allow you to simply calm down.

Go Here Now To Get Instant Access
https://www.morganknowlespublishing.com/free-book-offer

Introduction

Hi ladies, and welcome to The VISIBILITY Method. Thank you for choosing this book, or at least for reading this introduction and considering investing in yourself and this revolutionary approach to dealing with your anxiety. You are in the right place. You have been drawn here because either you or someone you know is struggling with anxiety issues. You can rest assured you will find comfort, reassurance, identification and practical techniques within these pages that will help you regain control of your life.

If you are a man wanting to support a female partner or relative, I truly admire that and commend you for doing a wonderful thing. This book will give you some insight into the reasons why some of us ladies struggle with anxiety disorders. If you are a woman who wishes to help a man with anxiety, or a guy looking for solutions, I have also written a version of this book specifically for men that will look at the masculine driving factors behind the illness.

This book is specifically aimed at women because, while anyone can suffer from anxiety disorders, men and women have many different pressures and experiences, so the approach to dealing with it must be specific. It is a fact that anxiety is more prevalent in women than men, and this is due to a number of factors which I will cover shortly.

According to a study conducted by the NHS in 2016, one in five women (20%) and one in eight men (12%) suffer from a common mental disorder such as anxiety or depression. Not only are women more likely to have anxiety, but they report their anxiety levels to be 24% higher than men.

"Anxiety does not empty tomorrow of its sorrows, but only empties today of its strength."

~ Charles Spurgeon (Donvito, 2021)

As the quote above says, anxiety drains our emotional and physical strength, but the feelings we have don't solve the problem itself, and we don't feel better the next day; in fact, the feeling is often a little worse. While emotionally charged matters of the mind are not always easy to understand or overcome, it doesn't mean they're impossible to come back from. Our feminine brains are complex, that's for sure - often because they constantly have so many things to deal with. They are linked to every aspect of our body because the signals from our brain tell us what to do or how to do something. They make us respond in the form of an action or an emotion, and it is so quick we barely recognise that our brain is telling us what to do...

But what if I told you that you CAN reprogramme your brain to respond differently?

For some women, this sounds like a crazy suggestion. Our emotions and actions are often triggered by other things, but it's always our brain that pushes the reaction button. While some reactions are natural, other actions are triggered by something that we have a negative experience with, and those are the instances we need to look out for. If you are already suffering in your mind, you might blow everything out of proportion rather than reacting rationally. This is a common but problematic response for women who feel anxious or depressed, but take it from me; it doesn't have to be like that!

In this book, we'll explore The VISIBILITY Method.

I know what you're thinking... What on earth is The VISIBILITY Method? And there's a simple answer to that question. It's a step-by-step method to help you cope with anxiety and depression by using Cognitive Behavioral Therapy (CBT) techniques. So many women feel unworthy and unseen, and this feeling is often at the core of anxiety and depression. The VISIBILITY Method helps you recognise your own self-worth because you are not invisible, and it's my mission to make you realize that you deserve visibility - simply for being you!

So many women have been diagnosed with Generalized Anxiety Disorder and are struggling to cope, but there seems to be very little help available. Medication is generally handed out too quickly, and while it is sometimes required, there are often other strategies to try first which may be more effective with most conditions. There are numerous symptoms of anxiety which we will cover shortly, and it's often difficult to pinpoint a direct cause, meaning that many women struggle to be diagnosed. Therefore, they are left struggling with their nerves, anxiety, and depression for long periods of time, only for a diagnosis to be made much further down the line. The point is, when it comes to mental health, it's best to find an answer sooner rather than later so that treatment can begin. In most cases, you need a diagnosis in order to treat the problem!

Many triggers can lead to anxiety disorders in women. We all experience pressures of responsibilities every day, and for women, in particular, those can be varied and relentless. Think about how many roles you try and fulfill daily - perhaps you are a mother, daughter, sister, wife, boss, employee, carer, friend etc. The list might go on and on. As women, we naturally tend to be nurturers and put the needs of others before ours, which can put us under a lot of stress.

Before we get into the method and techniques, let's start by taking a closer look at why some of us suffer from anxiety and what symptoms we might experience.

Causes of Anxiety in Women

Chemical imbalances - It may be in our biology that women are more likely to experience anxiety. Our brains contain chemicals called neurotransmitters, and there are two main categories. One makes us feel calm or happy (inhibitory) and the other produces sensations of excitement, stress or fear (excitatory). Men naturally have more serotonin, which is an inhibitory neurotransmitter, which could mean that women are more affected by changes in their environments as they are constantly looking for potential threats. When adrenaline levels are often raised (excitatory), the happy and calming chemicals reduce, leading to an oversensitive reaction to stimuli and resulting in anxiety.

Stress at work - We all know that work can be stressful for anyone, but women may have to deal with additional stressors such as discrimination (sexual or otherwise), harassment or inequality in the workplace.

Pressures of domestic responsibilities - Despite it being 2021, there is still a general expectation that even when in a relationship, women will do the majority (if not all) of the domestic chores in a household, including washing, cooking, cleaning, looking after the children etc. This puts tremendous pressure on women, particularly if they also have demanding jobs.

Societal pressures - There are many additional demands that women experience from their families and society. These relate to expected ways of behaving (getting married and having children by a certain age), types of employment deemed 'suitable,' plus ways of dressing and even speaking. To conform to these restrictions can cause stress, and if we choose to break the mold, we may have to deal with a backlash.

Hormones and stress - Yes, our hormones and their monthly changes due to our menstrual cycle can lead to additional stress. In fact, anything that causes significant, long-term stress can result in an anxiety disorder. For example, as women, we may be more emotionally affected by a relationship breakdown, a severe family argument, or a fight with a friend, which could cause increased anxiety levels.

Trauma - Any negative event such as being the victim of abuse (sexual, physical, verbal or psychological) can trigger anxiety. This may be an unresolved trauma from the past or a more recent event that you are finding difficult to process or deal with.

Symptoms of Anxiety in Women

The number and severity of symptoms of anxiety vary per person. You may experience one or two from this list or perhaps even all of them. Anxiety can affect us psychologically and physically, so there are symptoms that fit within these two categories.

- Uneasiness
- Constantly feeling tense
- Lack of concentration
- A fearful sensation
- Feeling irritable
- A desire to withdraw and isolate
- Feeling faint or dizzy
- Increased tiredness
- Heart palpitations (faster than usual or irregular heartbeat)
- Tense or achy muscles
- Shaking or trembling
- Suffering from a dry mouth
- Sweating more than usual
- Find it difficult to breathe
- Stomach pains
- Nausea
- Headaches or migraines
- Pins and needles
- Insomnia

Now that we've covered some of the science, let's get down to the nitty-gritty. This book isn't for everyone, but it's for YOU if you're a woman and:

· You're tired of your anxieties and depression holding you back.

· You suffer from negative feelings, but you're ready to overcome them.

· You are ready to challenge your belief systems and thinking patterns.

· You want to overcome your fears, move forward, and have a more positive mindset.

· You're ready to learn and take action to improve your life!

That's because throughout this book, you'll get to really know yourself, and you'll begin to understand the way that you think. Along with that awareness, you'll learn key CBT strategies to help you change your negative patterns and beliefs into positive ones. I believe that knowledge is power, and by making subtle changes, we can reprogramme the way we think and the messages our brain sends to us. You will take back control and learn to cope better, combatting your feelings of anxiety and depression along the way.

But that's not all...

This book doesn't stop there. At this point in the process, you'll explore further systems and strategies to help you grow into the real you – the happy, content, strong and amazing woman that I know you are already, even though right now, you may not see it yourself. You see, throughout my life, I've coped with many struggles myself, and I've supported loved ones who suffer from mental health issues, including schizophrenia and anxiety disorders. It bothers me that there's such a stigma surrounding this, and I strongly believe we need to talk more and break the cycle of ignorance.

Mental health and anxiety have played a huge role in my life. It's my mission to help other women find ways to cope and ease their symptoms so that they can overcome the constraints that prevent them from succeeding in everyday life the way they would like to. I've helped my partner overcome anxiety, and I've developed real coping mechanisms that have worked for both of us. I believe it's essential to focus on the now, rather than dwelling on the past or the future. Mental health doesn't just affect the sufferer, it impacts everyone involved in that person's life, and I recognise the effect this has on everyone. Such issues are deeply important to me, and I've written this book to share my knowledge and experience to help support you and other sufferers and let you know you are NOT alone!

Let me share with you some examples of female celebrity actresses who suffer from anxiety. Just because someone is rich and famous doesn't mean that they don't have the constant battle with negative thoughts, nagging doubts, irrational fears, etc. For example, Marilyn Monroe, Princess Diana, Amy Winehouse are known to have spoken about anxiety during their lifetimes. The singer and actress Miley Cyrus, actresses Kristen Stewart, Emma Stone, Kristen Bell, singer Ariana Grande and model Kate Moss, to name just a few, have also opened up during interviews about their struggles with anxiety.

Understanding and accepting ourselves is the key to understanding and accepting others. Anxiety and depression are often triggered by events in our lives that impact us. These events are often traumatic, even though we don't always realize it at the time. Getting to the root of the matter is key for recovery, so throughout this book I'm counting on you to be open and honest with yourself. For me, I had to deal with my parents separating for two years when I was just 8 years old, resulting in me living with grandparents during that time without really understanding what or why this was happening.

Anxiety and depression create a void within us and make us believe we're just not good enough at fulfilling our roles as mother, wife, daughter, friend, etc. If you get caught up in the void, it's difficult to escape, but you can learn to heal it, break the cycle and begin to feel whole again. By following this book and each chapter in turn, you will explore the core beliefs and thinking patterns that are at the heart of how you feel and react.

If you're tired of making excuses for yourself as you constantly sabotage your healing process, following this book may just surprise you. It's time to start living the way you *want* and stop living with the weight of the world on your shoulders. So many women shy away from mental health issues rather than proactively dealing with the issues. This book isn't the kind of book that encourages burying your head in the sand or ignoring problems. If this is you, it's time to make peace with yourself, and once we've truly explored the issue and pinpointed the root, you will be able to remain in the present, take back control, and live your limitless life. It's time to get those questions on general anxiety answered truthfully and adopt coping mechanisms that will last you a lifetime!

If you're ready to explore the power of Cognitive Behavioral Therapy, then you should head to Chapter 1, but before you go, consider this famous proverb:

> *"Just when the caterpillar thought the world was ending, he turned into a butterfly."*
> ~ Anonymous

Just like the caterpillar, you are so much more than you will ever know, until you go through your own transformation.

Are you ready to transform?

The world is waiting for you...

Chapter 1

Visualization - How You Start to Use Cognitive Behavioral Therapy Every Day

In this chapter, we are going to discuss an important topic, Cognitive Behavioral Therapy (CBT). You've probably heard this mentioned before, but you may not be entirely sure what it means or how it works. That's why I'm going to introduce the five core elements of CBT and discuss how it can help you by altering the way you think. We'll explore how CBT can help with many different disorders associated with mental health and talk about how it can be used as self-therapy, without drugs, to assist women suffering from anxiety.

What is Cognitive Behavioral Therapy?

Cognitive Behavioral Therapy (CBT) is a type of therapy known for helping you change the way you think or behave. It's a form of talking therapy that can help you make sense of and overcome a range of issues that are overwhelming you by sorting them into five core elements:

1. Situations

2. Emotions

3. Actions

4. Thoughts

5. Physical feelings

Let's look at each of these core elements, in turn, so we know exactly what each means and can see how they interconnect with one another.

Situations

Situations are certain sets of circumstances or surroundings that a person finds themselves in. In CBT, we look at how situations trigger negative emotions, thoughts or actions.

Emotions

Emotions are the feelings you experience instinctively. In CBT, we consider the emotions you feel as a result of your circumstances, relationships, mood, or the situations you're enduring. Certain situations or events can trigger emotions.

Actions

Actions are when we do something or the way we deal with something. We generally complete an action due to some other driving factor as we often respond to situations or emotions. In CBT practices, we explore the thing that causes the response.

Thoughts

As you know, thoughts are the ideas or opinions that suddenly occur in the mind. CBT looks at why we have those specific thoughts, especially negative ones or those that don't serve us in the best way.

Physical feelings

Physical feelings are the sensations that have a physical impact on us. It's the way our body reacts as a result of a driving factor. For example, people who suffer with stress and anxiety could feel sick or dizzy or may feel pains in their head or joints.

All of these core elements of CBT are interconnected, so each one affects the other. For example, if you're depressed, then your emotions are affected but it can also influence how you act and think, and vice-versa.

How is CBT different?

CBT is a type of psychotherapy. Psychotherapies are often seen as being powerful experiences that are responsible for improving social challenges, mental health and emotional challenges. Many people say that psychotherapies have changed their lives for the better. Although CBT falls under the psychotherapy umbrella, it is, however, very different in comparison to other psychotherapies available.

CBT differs as it is:

- **Collaborative**

CBT isn't about a therapist telling you how to solve your problems or difficulties; it's about them helping you find the solution yourself. The whole idea of CBT is to help you work out the best way to overcome your issues for yourself. It accepts that everyone is an individual, and what works for one person may not be the right path for another. This collaborative approach empowers you to realize that you already have all the answers within you, so when you learn the techniques, you can apply them consistently to solve future problems.

- **Pragmatic**

CBT is pragmatic because it helps you identify your own specific problems and encourages you to try and solve them. It enables you to deal with the issues in a realistic but practical way. You know yourself better than anyone, so you know your limits. If you have a hectic job, three kids and are a single mum, it would be unrealistic to suddenly decide to have a few hours a day of 'me time.' CBT helps you find logical answers.

· **Focuses on current problems**

CBT is concerned with the now rather than the past. It's important to consider how you think and act today and deal with that by taking action to improve your current situation. While accepting that the past is important, CBT doesn't work to resolve previous trauma. If you feel that past issues are significantly affecting you and blocking you from change, you may want to see an alternative therapy to address these first.

· **Highly structured**

As CBT is focused on your current problems, your attention is centered on the specific problems right now, and you set goals based on this. With other therapies, you tend to talk freely about your life, including previous events, but CBT is specifically structured to ensure you stay on topic.

CBT concentrates on negative thinking and helps prevent your destructive thought cycles. Negative thoughts become a habit over time, which means they increase and lead to further issues. We respond to those in either an unhelpful or helpful way, but the more negative your thinking patterns become, the more likely you are to become stuck in detrimental thought cycles. For instance, if a few things go wrong at the same time - you lose your job, and your relationship comes to an end - you start to feel that everything is going wrong for you. In truth, it's a series of unfortunate events, and there isn't a single cause; however, you may feel it's down to you. You could think you've lost your job because you're not good at your profession or people don't like you. You may also blame yourself for your relationship breakup and believe that you'll never have another decent job or meaningful connection. As a result, you feel down and isolate yourself – you don't even attempt to meet someone new or get another job.

CBT helps you gain perspective and assess why you're getting stuck in these negative cycles. With a clear mindset, there's no reason to think you'll never get a job or have another relationship due to past experiences. The important thing is putting things in perspective – many people lose their jobs on a daily basis for a variety of reasons. Many people also have relationships that break down, and that's often because the person isn't right for them. As you put things into a different context, you can start to manage your problems in a more pragmatic way, set goals based on what you want, and challenge yourself to achieve them. We'll cover negative thought patterns in more detail in Chapter 3, where we'll learn how to pinpoint and change them!

Who invented CBT?

The short answer is that American psychiatrist Aaron T. Beck is known to be the father of Cognitive Behavioral Therapy. He founded the psychotherapy approach in the 1960s. Beck has contributed significantly to psychotherapy, psychometrics, and psychopathology studies. He has also developed pioneering methods that are still used today to treat mental health disorders, such as anxiety and depression.

Beck coined the term 'automatic cognitions,' which are the basis for CBT methods. After discovering that these cognitions fell into three categories: negative ideas about the world, oneself and about the future, he began helping patients to consider their thoughts, put them into perspective, and as a result, improve how they felt and acted in light of these things. It was with his findings he was able to develop the key ideas behind CBT. Beck's research continued as he discovered that particular disorders were linked to distorted thinking, and how these thoughts impacted a person's core beliefs.

Beck continued his research over several years and has written or co-written 25 books and over 600 journal articles based in his field.

How to get rid of cognitive distortions

As women suffering from anxiety, we often imagine things are much worse than they actually are. That's why we've talked about perspective a lot in this chapter. Once we view something in a negative way, it can be really difficult to change how we see or think about it. This is a cognitive distortion, and as a result, our irrational or negative thinking can, in fact, escalate, which can affect the way we view everything.

Our thoughts often cause us to make assumptions, but when we are thinking irrationally, these assumptions are generally false and can impact other parts of our lives. Our behavior and mood can fall into a downward spiral, and we can become anxious and depressed as a result of this.

The good news is that you can fix your cognitive distortions. However, in order to do this, you need to be able to identify what your negative or irrational thoughts are. Only then can you start to put things into perspective and move forward.

Many women find that once they discover their cognitive distortions, it's the thoughts and opinions that often upset them rather than the situation itself. That's why it's important to work on how you think and perceive things. Countless women work with mental health specialists when assessing their cognitive distortions, but this is something you can practice yourself using CBT methods. Although, if you do feel you need some guidance or support, you should seek out a therapist to help you.

If you want to prevent negative thoughts, there are nine ways to reframe them. Over the next seven days, follow the activities below because identifying and dealing with your negative thought patterns is the basis for your CBT journey:

1. Check in with yourself

Checking in with yourself is a great way to consider how you are. This is the first way to reframe your negative thoughts. Most people don't tend to do this, but simply taking some time to ask yourself what's going on can have a positive impact. Take a few moments to check in with yourself and think about how you're feeling.

Ask yourself:

      a)   How am I really feeling today?
      b)   Am I focused on this task?
      c)   Do I have any physical symptoms?
      d)   If so, when did these symptoms begin?
      e)   Is my body feeling relaxed or tense?
      f)   Is anything impacting how I feel?

2. Identify your cognitive distortions

Discovering your cognitive distortions isn't always easy, but it's necessary so that you have an idea of which type of negative thoughts you're often having. In order to get to the bottom of this, you need to log your thinking patterns and the best way to do this is to keep or create a mood journal.

A mood journal is basically something you can use to log your thoughts and moods. You can then look at what you're thinking and consider why you're having those thoughts. This type of reflection is often referred to as metacognition.

<u>Steps to creating your mood journal</u>

i)   Write down your most noticeable thoughts in the exact way they pop into your head. Don't expand on this in any way; simply write down the thought.

ii)   Make the connection. Try linking those thoughts to a place or situation. If you're not finding this part easy, you can use these questions to work out any connections:

- *When and where were you when you had this thought for the first time?*
- *How many times has it occurred since then?*
- *What other thoughts do you have in similar situations? Are there any similarities to compare between them?*

iii)   Make a note of the emotions you experience with this particular thought. *What emotions do you feel when you have this particular thought and reflect on the situation?*

iv)   Keep completing your diary over a 7-day period.

v)   Once you reach the end of the week, it's time to group your thoughts together. For instance, if you think things like 'I never get offered career opportunities' or 'Nobody ever listens to me' or 'I always get left out,' those thoughts could be grouped together. This means you can look at how often these types of thoughts repeat in your mind, and you could also consider which thoughts cause you the most distress. This process will help you make sense of your thoughts and thought patterns.

3. Role reversal

When considering your thoughts, it's important to put them into perspective, and a role reversal allows you to do this. Doing this can help you see the gravity of your thoughts and how you view yourself.

Read through your thoughts and think about how you would respond if someone was saying these things about someone you love. *What would you say?*

Flip these thoughts and replace them with something more positive. For instance, if you feel you are not worthy of a promotion in your job, then imagine someone else was saying this about your loved one and argue their corner. Tell them exactly why they're worthy!

4. Where's the evidence?

When practicing CBT, it's important that you start to challenge your negative thought patterns. Negative thoughts are often opinion-based rather than being factual. If you don't have any evidence to support your negative thoughts, they may be unfounded and untrue.

This is similar to the role reversal step above, as here, you're looking for evidence that contradicts your negative thinking patterns. Most destructive thoughts are based on us criticizing ourselves, which is something that many women do. Such thoughts bring down our mood and do not serve us in any way.

Instead of being negative, make a list of positive or productive things you've done today. You may find you've done some things that show you are efficient, organized, loving, supportive and successful. Think about any positive comments you've received or what you accomplished when completing a specific task or activity. Perhaps your family thanked you for the lovely meal you made them, or a friend really appreciated your support with a problem they were having.

You should also make sure you separate opinions and facts, as you will notice that the majority of cognitive distortions are simply unfounded opinions that can't be evidenced. This can really help you when it comes to perspective!

5. Break down the labels

When you begin to identify the negative thought patterns, you'll start to see what labels you place on yourself. However, it's important that these labels never apply to you as a whole person. For example, if you view yourself as a failure, you don't fail at everything.

Pay close attention to the labels you are placing on yourself, and don't be afraid to challenge them – really focus on when you have done something well.

6. Don't generalize your cognitive distortions

This is something you'll have to work out, especially if you've already fallen deeply into negative thinking patterns. When something negative happens, many women take that one incident and apply it to everything they do and everyone they encounter. For example, just because you didn't lose the amount of weight you wanted to before going on holiday doesn't mean you will never lose it. You're overgeneralising a specific situation. If you identify these differences, you can reframe the situation in your mind.

Try the *opposite threes* technique...

The *opposite threes* technique means every time you find yourself overgeneralising, you think of three opposites to this event or situation. So, if you think you will never get a promotion, you need to identify times in your life when you've succeeded in your job – for example, to have a job already, you'll have succeeded in your interview. Think of some other ways in which you've done well or developed when it comes to your career. Focus on how you've contributed to your team or the organization.

7. Don't speculate

As human beings, we often make speculations, but as most of us have no psychic abilities, it's important to remember that we are simply assuming these things – they are not facts. Our speculations are often incorrect, as they stem from our insecurities of what others will be thinking about us or something we've done. Consider the quote below:

"Don't build roadblocks out of assumptions."
~ Lorii Myers, Targeting Success, Develop the Right Business Attitude to be Successful in the Workplace

This is exactly what speculations do... They build barriers that prevent us from moving forward and beyond. The only issue is, the barriers you build only hinder YOU, not anyone else.

Before you jump to any conclusions, you should take a reality check. Instead of dwelling on the things you think are happening or will happen, talk about them. Don't be afraid to ask for the opinions of others. For instance, if you feel you aren't performing well in your job, ask your manager for their input on your performance. If you feel your relationship isn't going so well, speak to your other half and see how they feel.

Doing this will help you review your situation, and it's likely that you'll find these feelings are linked to your own cognitive distortions. It will also set you at ease, because you'll have a starting point to work from. Maybe your manager will agree that you need to develop in a specific area but suggest something you can do to improve. Your partner may set your mind at ease, or they may open up to you if there is something on their mind or upsetting them. Then you can again work out a way forward.

Of course, when you ask for another person's opinion, there's always a risk that they aren't being entirely truthful, but that's for you to assess. You can always ask for more than one person's input. The idea is to help to identify which of your negative thinking patterns aren't based on facts.

8. Work on the 'shoulds'

Using the term 'should' is a common negative distortion. Thinking about how you 'should' act or the things you 'should' do, isn't always accurate. There are many things many people feel they 'should' do but don't, and by using that term, they are setting themselves up to fail.

What if we did something completely wild?

What if we changed our 'shoulds' and replaced them with alternative language? For instance, we could replace the 'should' with 'could.' So instead of saying, 'I should go to the gym this morning,' say, 'I could go to the gym this morning.' Alternative phrases we could use include:

It'd be nice if...

It'd be great if I...

I'd love to...

I'd really like to...

Using these phrases can improve your mood and really change your perspective. It takes away the pressure that the term 'should' places on you, which improves how you feel – it feels more like a choice than a reprimand.

9. Cost-effectiveness

When considering cost, we're usually considering the cost associated with the benefits of our decisions. Every decision we make costs us in some way. The payment isn't always money, but it could cost us in terms of harm.

Here, you need to take the negative thoughts you've identified and work out the benefits and drawbacks of each thought. You can physically draw this out as pros and cons lists on a piece of paper or in your mood journal. Think about how each thought helps or hinders you...

If you find that some thoughts do more harm than good, you can visually see this, and therefore you will feel justified in tackling them. Any thoughts that do not best serve you need to be challenged.

Some of your thinking patterns may benefit you, and it's useful to recognise those too. That's because they'll serve you in a positive way, and if so, it will help you see how you can make the most of such thinking patterns.

Now we've looked through 9 steps to reframe your cognitive distortions, you will understand more about negative thinking patterns and how such untrue opinions and assumptions can affect your mood. Reframing your cognitive distortions takes time, hard work and dedication, but it's an important part of healing yourself. This is the first step to improving your mood and eradicating negative thoughts, but often such problems run much deeper than that. In Chapter 3, we'll focus on this in a more in-depth and proactive way. However, before that, we're going to focus on goal setting and what inspires you in Chapter 2.

What disorders can CBT help with?

CBT addresses the negative ways we think (cognitive therapy) and behave (behavior therapy). With that in mind, it can assist with a range of disorders and is widely used for anxiety disorders.

A lot of research has been conducted in relation to CBT, and it is said to be effective when treating many different mental health disorders. These include panic disorders, phobias, generalized anxiety disorder and social anxiety disorder. Research also shows it's effective in treating acute stress disorder, post-traumatic stress disorder (PTSD), illness anxiety disorder and obsessive-compulsive disorder (OCD). In addition, the techniques can also be used in the treatment of separation anxiety.

Now that you're beginning to come to terms with CBT and how it can help, you're probably wondering what this book has in store for you. As anxiety is a major factor in the lives of so many women, we'll be focusing on that in Chapter 2, alongside goal setting, forming a routine and looking at how we can feel inspired. Throughout the rest of the book, we'll be delving deeper into negative thinking patterns, changing and challenging our core belief system, and discovering how to stay present but move forward, away from past events. We'll also be exploring ways to eradicate worries, deal with anger, loving yourself and others while also focusing on acceptance and an acknowledgement of tomorrow.

This book is about to head on an epic CBT journey, and I want you to embark upon this journey with me. *Are you ready for The VISIBILITY Method?*

Chapter 2

Intention - Turning Your Anxiety Into A Routine

In this chapter, we're really going to keep the focus on anxiety. We're going to talk about goal setting and time management and how they can be used to overcome anxiety. You'll soon learn how to turn your anxiety into a routine that suits you, and in turn, it will inspire you and improve your life.

Goal setting is a useful tool used when dealing with anxiety disorders. In Chapter 1, we talked a lot about perspective, and goal setting helps you to put things into perspective and prioritize too. We'll explore this in detail throughout this chapter.

Although you perhaps feel really busy and rushed all the time, the more structure you have in your day, the less you have to think and plan how you're going to spend time, which means you have less opportunity to get caught up in your thoughts. Managing our time can help with productivity, too, and that's why we'll also focus on this throughout this chapter.

In addition, we'll talk about how you can create a journal to help with your anxiety.

The rationale behind why setting goals can help with anxiety

Goal setting is great for women who have anxiety. That's because goals give you the opportunity to change by imagining your life without anxiety. As you identify where you want to go and the steps you need to get there, you can monitor your progress.

There are many benefits of setting goals:

· They give you focus and direction – you have something to aim for. Setting a clear goal can push you in the right direction, especially if you break it down into smaller steps, so you can mark off your achievements as you go. It's recommended that you create SMART goals. We'll discuss those later in this chapter.

· They can help keep you motivated - feeling like you've accomplished something helps keep you inspired. If you're setting goals but also setting smaller steps along the way, the more you achieve and the more accomplished you will feel. It's easy to lose your motivation, and that's why your goals need to be measurable. Sometimes, things don't always go your way, and you must learn to accept that. Just go back to your initial goals when you face a setback and adjust them to the current situation. Remember, setbacks are part of long-term success and creating new goals to overcome obstacles is a great way to break down barriers and ensure change is sustainable.

· They allow you to monitor your progress and performance – goals are great for allowing you to measure change as you log a long or short-term goal and list the steps you need to take to achieve it. As you tick off each step, you can keep track of your advancements and achievements. If your goals are bound by timescales, it can help you check you're on target to deliver the end goal on time.

· They hold you accountable – goals can effectively hold you to account. Once you write down your objective, you've put your intention in writing, and you should view this as a contract with yourself. You're then clear with the expectations placed on you, and if you check your goals every day, you are reminded daily of what is required. If you set timescales, this also holds you to 'when' each step should be completed. The smaller steps you take to reach your end goal can be ticked off along the way, which will also keep you on track!

· They provide you with a sense of achievement – sometimes goal setting is overwhelming, especially if your goals are big. The simplest way to keep going is to set both long and short-term goals so as to build your sense of achievement on a regular basis. Through doing this, your self-esteem will also improve significantly along the way. The key is to set goals that are achievable. You should never set yourself up to fail! You will feel accomplished as you tick off each step along the way.

· They allow you to prioritize the things that are most important to you – if you set clear goals, it can become easier to prioritize what's next for you. Deciding on your priorities can be tricky, so the best thing to do is write out your goals so you can see them, then organize them in order of urgency and importance. Focus on your urgent and important goals first, urgent only goals next, followed by important goals, and finally, any other goals that are not urgent, nor important, but you still want to achieve them.

· They provide clarity – there's no denying that goals give us clarity. The goal you are aiming to achieve, and the steps along the way will be specific and clear, so you'll know exactly what to do to achieve it. Sometimes, our objectives change, so don't worry if you look through your goals and find that one or two are no longer applicable – simply alter them. Your goals must provide clarity, but they should also be kept up-to-date and relevant.

· They prevent you from feeling overwhelmed – goals can prevent us from thinking that everything is too much. If you aren't feeling 100% or are particularly anxious, the goals you have set indicate what you have to do. This means you don't have to make decisions about what you want to achieve; you simply have to follow the steps. Also, having a big goal can be somewhat intimidating, but when you break your goals down into smaller steps, it removes the pressure and makes them much easier to achieve. Nobody is expecting you to achieve a significant goal in one day. However, you will prevent feeling overwhelmed if you gradually tick off your smaller steps as you work towards the ultimate objective.

· They give you purpose – many people see goals as their purpose in life. Basically, it's your mission to follow the steps of each goal and eventually achieve it. This gives you something clear to work towards and makes overcoming any barriers much easier. It tells you what to do and when to do it and gives you a sense of meaning. Goal setting gives you the desire you need to achieve your mission. Part of this is because goals are specific and therefore, you know what and why you're aiming for this particular outcome.

All of the benefits listed above can help women who suffer from anxiety. An anxious person worries about many things, so having something positive to aim for can help them move forward. Breaking down goals into smaller sections makes goal setting much simpler and much less daunting.

Many women fail when it comes to goal setting, simply because they set big goals that take a long time to complete. This sets them up to fail as they don't see any progress, and for someone with anxiety, that can be catastrophic. It means that often, they give up and end up feeling even worse as they believe they've failed again. You should never set yourself up to fail!

We talked about CBT in the previous chapter, and in the early stages of CBT, we look at your thinking patterns. The good thing about setting goals, is that although you initially have to think about the goals you want to accomplish, you don't have to constantly worry about them as you work to achieve them. When we have specific and achievable goals, it can prevent us from overthinking. We have clear steps or instructions to follow, and therefore, we don't need to think too much about the task and how we'll complete it; we simply need to get it done. Overthinking is a common trait in women who suffer from anxiety, but it actually makes anxiety worse.

Why overthinking causes anxiety to become even worse and how to combat this

When we overthink, we often worry and as a result, we experience feelings of distress that lead to further depression and anxiety. We can begin to lose control, especially if we don't deal with this. But it's not always that easy!

Overthinkers typically find themselves overcome by their obsessive thoughts, but it becomes so out of control, it brings on feelings of self-loathing, self-blaming and regret. While everyone overthinks something occasionally, some women find that they can't stop their train of thought when it comes to this.

Overthinking involves our inner monologue and has two components:

· Worrying

· Ruminating

Worrying involves negative thoughts around our perceptions of what may or may not happen in the future. Worrying thoughts are a drain on your energy, and they cause distress because they prevent you from doing what you want to do. Small worries can spiral out of control as we overthink things so that they become much larger. As women, we often worry more about other people than we do ourselves. For example, suppose you have a child, and they are reported to have started demonstrating behavior issues in school. As you are at work or at home going about your daily routine, your mind may be worrying about what this could lead to. Will they become impossible to control? Maybe they will get expelled from school. Perhaps they have started associating with the wrong people and will get involved in drugs. They won't be able to get a job... It could lead to crime... And so on. However, the reality could be simple, such as they find lessons boring because they are very intelligent or need glasses and act out because they cannot see the subject matter properly.

Ruminating involves over-analysing every detail of your life and replaying it over and over. It can lead to developing eating disorders, depression and anxiety. Ruminating may become an obsession, and we may begin to show regret (*I shouldn't have done that),* or begin to demonstrate feelings of self-blaming (*It's my fault he/she left me),* or self-loathing (*If I hadn't been so stupid/skinny/overweight, he/she'd have stayed).* These thoughts or beliefs then have a knock-on effect, and that's how anxiety, depression and eating disorders can develop or escalate. It's a vicious thought cycle.

It's important to remember that such thoughts do not serve you best. Overthinking is something that can deter you and hold you back. If you find yourself overthinking (repeating events over and over in your mind), tell yourself to 'Stop!' Psychotherapist Reuben Berger, noted in Made for Minds (2020), suggests saying this aloud, as it's more authoritative and effective. He recommends the *Thought Stopping Technique,* in which you begin to recognise your overthinking and tell yourself aloud to stop. This technique aims to condition you to break free from this negative loop that comes with rumination and worrying. He states that consistency is key here!

Why time management can help with anxiety

While time management comes easily for some people, especially busy women who are used to juggling family, home and work lives, for people with anxiety, time management can be much more challenging. The very thought of time management can trigger stress and anxiety responses. However, before you make a firm decision that this isn't for you, you need to read through this section. We will explore a few ways to improve your time management skills, and if managed correctly, it can actually help reduce anxiety.

Many women find that good time management allows them to focus on a particular task, one at a time, so they don't become overwhelmed. The best approach is to make a list of the things you need to do and prioritize each task. You can then use time-blocking techniques to allocate time slots to focus on and complete your tasks. When you do this, it can reduce anxiety as you've put your priorities in order and you're focusing on the most urgent or important matter first.

When you manage your time effectively, you are providing a structure to work from. Without structure, you are left with too many opportunities to ponder how to use all the time you have. Many women spend too long planning what to do or thinking/worrying about it, but this is a negative cycle of wasting time that you don't want to get stuck in. If you allocate two hours in the morning to a specific task, but your priorities suddenly change and another task becomes more important, don't be afraid to swap around your schedule for the day. Being flexible and open to change is a good thing as sometimes, if we try to force ourselves to complete a task but are not feeling up to it, the standard of our work could be substandard. Time management works best when you are working at your highest capacity, so take that into consideration too.

When you suffer from anxiety, the best thing you can do is develop a routine that works for you. To do this, you should:

- Ensure you've given yourself enough time to complete the tasks.

- Be flexible and allow for changes.

- Take regular breaks to ensure you can keep yourself energized with snacks and refreshments.

Time management is a great tool to reduce your anxiety, and you should commit to this consistently for several weeks if you want to see improvements. It's also important that you are kind to yourself. If you are having a particularly bad day, try to get on with as many things on your to-do list as you can, but don't beat yourself up about it. As long as it's not a daily occurrence, simply accept you've had a bad day and move on. Tomorrow will be much better! Dwelling only makes your anxiety worse, and it's pointless fixating on situations we can't control. This doesn't serve us!

The most important thing to do is develop a schedule that suits you best, and sometimes this means you need to tweak it.

The best way to set goals

We've mentioned setting goals already, but now it's time to do this. The most effective way to set goals is to create SMART goals. Setting SMART goals allows you to focus your efforts, clarify ideas and use your time in the best possible way. They help you achieve what you want in life. You may have already heard of the acronym SMART, but let's start at the beginning, just in case.

SMART means:

· **Specific** – your objectives should be as specific as possible for clarity. You should really think about what you want to accomplish, why this goal is important, which resources will be used, who is involved, and where it's located or taking place.

· **Measurable** – your objectives should be measurable so that you can track your performance and progress. Having measures in place can also help you stay focused and motivated. All measurable goals should consider how long/much something is, how many, and you should also think about how you will know when you've accomplished your target. For example, if you want to lose weight, set an achievable goal of 2lbs per week, which is measurable by weighing yourself each week.

· **Achievable** – we've talked about how we can avoid setting ourselves up to fail, and this is your opportunity to formulate your goals in a way that sets you up for success. Make your objectives achievable and line yourself up for that win! In order for your goal to be attainable, it has to be possible and not out of reach. Setting an achievable goal will help you accomplish it. Think carefully about how feasible the goal is based on the various constraints you may face (financial, time, knowledge, ability, etc.) as you strive for success.

· **Relevant** – all your objectives should be relevant to your life. Make sure that the goal matters to you (not just that you're doing it to please your family or partner) and that it's also in accordance with your other goals. Achieving your objectives can be a great feeling, but only if they are genuinely important to you. You can ask yourself a number of questions to examine the significance of each goal. Consider if the goal is worthwhile, if it's the right time, and if it's suitable. This can help you determine whether it's relevant or needs adjusting.

· **Time-bound** – all objectives should have a timescale attached to them, so that you know when the goal should be completed. Be as honest as possible and ask yourself: When can I complete this goal? What can I do six months/weeks from now? Also, consider what you can make a start on today.

There's no doubt that SMART is an important, effective tool when you're goal setting. It helps guarantee motivation, clarity and focus. Anyone can use SMART goals, and the way they are written ensures that they set us up for success in the future. Setting SMART goals can help you in many different areas, and they can also help you live a happier, more successful and fulfilled life.

How to set a goal and mean it

You may set goals and have every intention of seeing them through initially, but you may lack the motivation to keep going. It's really important to stay consistent when dealing with your goals, and here are five steps you should follow:

1. Pick one of your goals to focus on first, as this will prevent you from becoming overwhelmed. Only move to the subsequent one once you've completed the previous one. Don't worry if your goals are interconnected; simply check the objectives off when you move onto the next.

2. Write your goal down. Once it's down on paper, it's like a contract. Ensure it's broken down into smaller steps, sign it, and display it somewhere, so it catches your attention on a daily basis.

3. It's easy to fulfill goals you feel passionate about, so although you should prioritize your goals, you should also consider which goals you really want to achieve. If you don't feel like you want to achieve a specific goal, the likelihood is, you won't achieve it. Fulfilling goals takes motivation and passion!

4. Be positive but also strict with yourself – ensure you stay persistent. You must push/motivate yourself into achieving your goals and be a tough taskmaster – don't let yourself off the hook so easily. Keep working towards your objective, and remind yourself why you want to achieve it. Remember, the more steps you tick off, the more positive steps you are taking towards your achievement of this goal. Persistence and continuity are key here. Although you need to be patient and accepting of yourself in some cases, don't give up. Keep going and striving towards that goal.

5. Measure the improvements. For example, if your overall goal is to reduce your anxiety, be sure to test your anxiety levels and consider how they've improved in light of your goal. In order to stay motivated, we need to see results, and your progress will show you that you are capable of making a difference.

Journaling for anxiety

If you suffer from anxiety, journaling is highly recommended; and for most women, this is an enjoyable experience. Many of us kept diaries when we were younger, and we tend to be a bit more expressive than men when writing about personal matters. Think of it as if you are confiding in a best friend. It's a great tool to help you reduce any feelings of distress and improve your anxiety levels. Overall, it can increase your well-being.

Journalling isn't difficult as there are not really any rules or limitations. There are several ways in which one can do this. The first thing you should decide when journaling is the frequency. Will you be journalling:

a) Weekly?

b) Daily?

c) As and when it's needed?

This is something only you can decide, but in order to get into the habit, it's best to do this daily so that journalling becomes part of your routine. It will also be useful during CBT practices too as it helps you log your thoughts and feelings, which can reduce the anxiety you feel. Journalling is a powerful tool that also empowers you because it encourages action!

The ultimate goal of journaling is to get your worries down on paper. It's only then that you can break them down and problem solve, resolving any issues you log or encounter.

You can begin journaling by:

· Taking 5-15 minutes and jotting down what's on your mind. Ensure you stay in the present, and write what is happening right now, as well as any concerns you have.

· Review and reread what you've written. Be sure to explore your options and reflect on the concerns you have. Consider these questions:

> o Is there anything you can do to change things right now?
>
> o Could things be different?
>
> o Is change likely, and how do you know?
>
> o What fears are you experiencing, and how can you make it a less negative experience?
>
> o How likely is it that what you're worried about will happen? How do you know this, and are you sure?
>
> So what's the ideal outcome for you?
>
> o Is there any way that your current circumstances can create an even better outcome?

Questioning your thoughts and actions like this are really useful steps because it's all part of challenging your thinking patterns and thought processes. Although we've mentioned this already in Chapter 1, Chapter 3 is dedicated to taking it further.

It's time to delve deep and change the way you think! This will take strength and preparation, as we consider a plan to change those negative patterns that are making you miserable and unproductive.

Chapter 3

Switch - How You Pinpoint and Change Harmful Thoughts

Now you've learned all about goal setting and time management, and how to do this effectively to soothe your anxiety, you're now ready to focus on negative thinking patterns. In this chapter, we're going to work on changing the way you think, as this can have a positive impact on your anxiety. This is because constant worrying holds you back, and when you alter or challenge this, your mind allows you to start making progress.

The VISIBILITY Method on How to Cope with Anxiety is all about rising to the challenge and breaking down barriers.

We've already touched on negative thinking patterns in Chapter 1, but that barely scratched the surface. Our thinking patterns are very complex in nature, and in order to gain a strong level of understanding, we'll be exploring the following within this chapter:

- The 11 different thinking patterns

- What you can and can't control

- Focusing on what you CAN do

- Looking at what you do have, not what you don't

- Focusing on the now (more in Chapter 5)

- Distinguishing between what you need and what you want

- Emotional regulation

- Being assertive

Each of these points relates to negative thinking patterns, but it's only as we come to learn about them that we'll begin to have a true picture of our own thinking patterns.

It's time to begin transforming your thoughts, and in turn, you'll start to change your life and improve your general well-being, as well as it having a positive impact on your anxiety.

"Positive thinking will let you do everything better than negative thinking will."
~ Zig Ziglar (Brainy Quote)

As Zig Ziglar suggests in the quote above, positive thinking allows us to do better, but when you're in a negative mindset, this doesn't happen. If you can change just one or two thoughts soon, you'll notice a big difference in your life.

Let's do this!

The 11 different thinking patterns

In Chapter 1, we discussed cognitive distortions, but to be able to identify them, we need to fully understand what they are. Some of the different thinking patterns overlap with each other, and some of the concepts we've covered in Chapter 1, but we've sorted them into the most common categories below:

1. Dichotomous Thinking (sometimes referred to as black-and-white thinking) is when we don't read between the lines and simply accept that something is either good or bad, but nothing in between. Thinking in an all-or-nothing way is counterproductive as it encourages us to ignore the things that are more complex. For example, you want to diet because you feel fat and unattractive. Even as you lose weight and people compliment you, you still feel fat because you haven't reached your target weight yet.

2. Overgeneralization is when we take a single negative event and make it one of our universal truths of life. For instance, if you do something incorrectly: let's say you follow a recipe, but it doesn't turn out as planned. You then turn that one occurrence into believing that you're not a good cook because your recipes *always go wrong.*

3. Emotional Reasoning is when we believe the unfounded claims that we make about ourselves. For instance, we feel like nobody likes us, and we begin to believe it even though there is no evidence to suggest it is true.

4. Fortune-Telling is when we predict something negative is going to happen, before anything actually does. This links to the earlier example of the mum who worried about and imagined exclusion and a life of crime for her child after some behavioral issues in school. Such pessimistic ideas impact how we feel and reflect on our behavior. We begin to worry and fret over issues we don't need to, as there's no reason to. Not many people have actual fortune-telling abilities, so this thinking pattern can cause a lot of unnecessary stress and anxiety.

5. Mind-Reading is similar to fortune-telling, except, in this case, we make assumptions that we know and understand the thoughts of another person. As women, we may feel that we know our partner or family members well, so we might be quite confident that we are correct in our theories. However,

this can reflect poorly on us because, in hindsight, we never truly know what is going on in the mind of another.

6. Labeling is when we attach unnecessary labels to ourselves or others, which, again, are often unfounded and irrelevant. Once we do this, it's impossible to see beyond the label, and we become inflexible as we can't see that person or ourselves in a different light. We may inherit labels from other people, such as '*My dad always told me I was terrible with money.*' We spend our lives believing them and turning them into self-fulfilling prophecies rather than proving them wrong.

7. Minimizing is when we ignore or discount the positives in a situation. For example, imagine that something really great happens; let's say you run your first park run and come 10th. You've been training for months, but rather than celebrating your achievement, you downplay the event because you weren't first. Celebrating any successes, no matter how big or small, is important. It shows whether we value ourselves or not.

8. Magnification is when you turn everything into a catastrophe by blowing it out of proportion. It's when you take something that isn't so bad but then make it out to be the worst thing ever. For example, you may have heard people say things like, '*If I don't get those shoes, I'll die.*' They won't really die if they don't get a pair of shoes, and on a larger scale, a person could say things like '*I'm dying from embarrassment.*' The point is that this is all dramatized and exaggerated. By doing this, you are only causing distress for yourself.

9. Moral Imperatives are something you'll recognise from Chapter 1 when we talked about avoiding using the word 'should.' Others are 'shouldn'ts,' 'musts,' and 'mustn'ts.' These words put pressure on us to behave in a certain way. Try to eradicate using these moral imperatives and replace them with the phrases we looked at in Chapter 1:

I'd like to...

I'd love to...

It'd be nice if I could...

10. Personalization is when you make things about yourself when they are not. This could be something like blaming yourself for something that's beyond your control, such as the behavior of your partner at a family event ('*I shouldn't have made them go*'), or taking things personally when they are not aimed or intended for you.

11. Mental Filter is when you only see the negative aspects of an experience, so you overlook the positive and neutral aspects. For example, if you write a letter or email to someone and after you've sent it, you realize you've made a couple of mistakes with punctuation, and as a result, it's all you can think about.

In Chapter 1, you were asked to keep a mood journal to make a log of your negative thoughts. You were also provided with the tools to reframe them. Now you've learned about the 11 different thinking patterns, go back to your journal and see if you can see any correlations or tendencies when it comes to your own thoughts. *Which negative thinking patterns do you use most often?*

Until we can recognise what our negative thoughts are, and which category they come under, we can't possibly overcome our issues.

Now let's look at further advice so you can begin to move forward when it comes to negative and harmful thinking patterns.

What you can and can't control
Many women focus on the things they can't control rather than the things they can. You have to accept that some things happen in life that you simply don't have control over.

We all like to be in control, but there are occasions when this can be taken too far. There are external things that occur, that we simply can't control and yet we tend to focus on them, which only causes worry and distress. Sometimes, we just have to accept that we can't control everything and concentrate on what we do have power over. Sometimes, we can use the things we can control as a damage-limitation tool.

If you find you're worrying about things, but you have no control over them, there are some things you can do:

1. Consider what you can control

Take a few moments to examine your situation and identify the things you can and can't control. Even though you may not be able to prevent something from happening, you can plan ahead and prepare for it. It's the same when it comes to another person – you can't control a person's behavior, but you can control how you respond to it.

In order to do this, you have to acknowledge that there are some things you can't control. You can always manage your own attitude and effort, so use this to put energy into the things you can control. If you do this, you'll handle the situation much more effectively.

2. Concentrate on your influence

You have an influence on circumstances and people. Even though you cannot force things to go your way, you are entitled to provide your opinion. To have the best influence, you should focus on changing your behavior and ensure you're a good role model. You should also have healthy boundaries. If you have an opinion, feel free to share in a respectful way but show recognition of the barriers – it's not always down to you to fix a person or situation.

3. Know your fears

As much as we all want to say, 'I'm not afraid of anything,' we shouldn't ignore the fact that we all have fears. Knowing what yours are and accepting that those are your fears can strengthen your position. Think about what you're most afraid of, what you worry about happening and any situation that you doubt your ability to cope with. Now, take each of these and ask yourself, 'What's the worst that could happen as a result?' As mentioned in the negative thinking patterns discussed earlier in this chapter, sometimes we catastrophize the outcome, but the chances are that the worst outcome is actually not as bad as you think. The problem here is we spend so long telling people 'I can't...' that we don't assess situations effectively. If you can handle the worst-case scenario, you can handle anything in between.

4. Use ruminating and problem solving to overcome obsessive thoughts

For example, if you're constantly replaying events or conversations in your head, you should aim to resolve the problem. First, consider if your thinking is productive... What are the benefits of solving this problem? If there are some benefits, you can resolve the issue by working on solutions and increasing your chances of success.

If you decide that there are no benefits that serve you if you resolve the problem, then you need to stop ruminating as you're wasting your time. You should acknowledge that your thoughts aren't productive, and you should do something productive that takes your focus and distracts you for a while (like exercise or a specific small task).

5. Develop a stress management plan

There are a few things you need to do in order to take care of yourself. These include a healthy diet, exercise, drinking plenty of water and getting the sleep you need. If you manage your stress too, you'll find that you can operate in a more efficient way.

Create a plan to destress and take part in healthy stress relievers. Activities could include:

- Spending time with friends
- Taking time for your hobby
- Meditation
- Having a hot bath

Ensure you pay close attention to your stress levels and how you cope with any distress you face. Sometimes people begin to use unhealthy ways to cope, including drinking too much alcohol, substance misuse, or complaining to other people regularly. Keep it positive!

6. Inspire yourself with encouraging affirmations

Affirmations are a healthy, positive way to start the day well, and you can use them to boost your energy throughout the day too. Let's face it, if you begin the day with a pessimistic 'I hope it isn't too cold today,' you're already using a negative to complain about the weather. If it's warm, you won't celebrate this fact, and remember, you have no control over the weather. Positive affirmations should remind you that you can handle any situation you are not in control of, and if you can control the situation, it's down to you to make it happen. If the weather is cold, you should be reminding yourself that 'I can handle the cold weather' and you can make something happen. If you want to have a good day, tell yourself that you'll make it so!

Focusing on what you CAN do

We have a habit of focusing on the things we cannot do, rather than the things we can do. Even though we look at our own lives and think about the things we want to change, we don't always take the action required. Sometimes, we don't take action because of fear. This is not necessarily because the change itself is scary;

it's because we continue to complete our everyday habits without thinking about them, and making a change would mean we're taking a risk. We could fail, or we could give up.

Our actions are often conditioned or limited from when we are a child, continuing well into adulthood. There are things we may feel we can't do because of one reason or another. For instance, there are things we can't do because we have no money. Sometimes there are things we don't do because others dictate it. For example, we may feel we shouldn't do something because of certain beliefs we have inherited from our parents. Of course, there are laws that we abide by, but we have a lot of choices too, so next time, if you think you 'can't,' ask yourself, why? Is it really that you can't because it's not possible, or is it due to some other reason? If there are some barriers to overcome, but it's still 'possible,' then remember, it's not that you can't do something; it's just that you may have some obstacles to surmount first.

If you want to move closer to the life you've always dreamed of living, you need to focus on the things you can do. We don't always get second chances or do-overs, and our lives continue whether we give them permission or not. We do, however, get to choose what matters the most to us, and we can decide what to put our energy into. These choices – the things we can choose or decide, are what we should focus on.

If you train yourself to focus your energy on the things you can control, it will change your life and the way you view the world. You'll find that you start to alter your belief systems – you'll even begin to believe in yourself and build confidence in your own decisions and choices. Take the first step – take control of the things you can control and shift your focus only to the things you can do, as the things you can't don't matter.

Look at what you do have, not what you don't

So many women do not feel content with the things they have and are too busy thinking about what they don't have. This is particularly apparent for anxiety sufferers, as they tend to be concerned with how everyone else is feeling rather than working on themselves. If you find that this sounds like you, I want you to remember; you are lucky to have those things you have already. You're lucky if you have a spouse, a home, a car, a family, friends, a job, nice clothes, spare cash... I could go on. My point is, we should pay more attention to the things we already have, rather than what we don't.

Take a moment to think about everything you have that you should feel good about. Why not write down the things you have that you are thankful for?

Now, I'm not suggesting that you shouldn't have dreams and goals. If there's something you don't have that you really want, you should set goals so you can achieve it. By setting goals, you're taking practical and proactive action because you're fixing an intention. If you are simply pondering or obsessing with the things you lack, without planning how to succeed or achieve them, you are wasting your time and energy. Before you even consider wanting something you don't have, you should first be thankful for the things you do have. That's why I suggested writing a list of the things you are grateful for because sometimes we need to remind ourselves.

Now, if you find yourself spending a lot of time thinking about what others have, try to focus on that list of things you do have. You see, you have permission to be selfish. You should be focusing on the things you have and nurture them.

For example:
- Put energy into your relationships and build intimacy with your loved ones. You deserve it, and so do they.

· Your dreams and desires are YOURS, so don't neglect these. Work on achieving them in a practical and proactive way by setting goals, as we've already mentioned.

· Don't be afraid to give yourself time when you need it. This could be time to think, assess your situation, meditate or exercise. If you have dependent children, speak to your partner, a friend or a family member about childcare arrangements to give you some uninterrupted time.

· Don't look for validation or embrace guilt. We sometimes feel like we need our actions validated or feel guilty for spending time on ourselves. Stop! Don't even go there because you don't ever need validation, and you should never feel guilty for doing something just for yourself.

· Practicing doing something for you is the key. The more you do it, the more you value yourself, and the more it becomes a habit. It's a positive habit because it leads to a happy life. Recognise what you want, your feelings, and consider how the things you do serve you!

When you focus on what you have, you should also take some time to focus on the real you. Sometimes, it's impossible to know what we want in life because we don't spend enough time contemplating it and sometimes, we lose sight of who we really are. This is particularly the case when we are playing the simultaneous and demanding roles of mother, wife, executive, daughter, etc. Ensure you build a strong relationship with yourself and ascertain what you really want in life. If you are stuck in negative thought patterns, you may feel uncertainty about your own identity, and in this case, spending time just for you is important.

If you really want to get to know the real you and develop that relationship, you need to nurture yourself. Women who suffer from anxiety tend to neglect self-care, and yet, when they introduce this into their lives, they usually see positive changes in themselves. That's exactly why it's okay to be selfish from time to time, as we all deserve to feel good about ourselves, and we should also demonstrate that we value ourselves too. Self-care is a great way to build a connection with yourself and it's a great idea at this stage to create a self-care plan.

A self-care plan ensures you are not neglecting your basic needs: sleep, exercise, relaxation and nutrition. It's an opportunity to focus and connect with yourself, and it's a great way to destress too. To get started with your self-care plan, you should:

1. Ensure that you include plenty of energy-boosting foods in your diet.

2. Try meditation and mindfulness.

3. Make time for exercise, even if it's just 10 minutes each day.

4. Continue with your mood journal – this can be written, or you can draw your feelings.

5. Read a book for leisure.

6. Plan to spend at least 2 hours outdoors, preferably with nature, each week.

7. Make time to practice gratitude and self-compassion.

All of the things above can really help you make positive changes in your life. Many women often report that the more positive they feel, the more they make positive things happen in their life. You've got nothing to lose by giving this a try, but make sure you go all in. You can't expect positive things to happen if you have a negative mindset, so working on your core beliefs is key here. We'll discuss these further in Chapter 4.

Focusing on the now

Chapter 5 is all about staying present, but it's relevant right here, in this chapter too, so let's touch on this briefly. So many women who suffer from anxiety worry about the past and fret about the future. However, the only thing we should all be concerned with right now is the present. Anxiety is often escalated by the thought of too many outcomes of what today will bring, and it's important to anchor yourself to the moment so that you don't begin to feel overwhelmed. In truth, we sometimes get so caught up in the *idea* of making a decision that we end up making no decision – this just wastes time! It's completely counterproductive.

Before we move on, let me draw your attention to three great quotes that are here to remind you of the importance of staying present. The quotes are from three different people who all appreciate the importance of staying present.

The first quote is to remind you that we shouldn't be concerned with the past because we can't do anything about that:

"I don't know who my grandfather was; I am much more concerned to know what his grandson will be."

~ Abraham Lincoln (Kumar, 2018)

The second quote is here to ground you and remind you of what you have right now:

"Be happy in the moment, that's enough. Each moment is all we need, not more."

~ Mother Teresa (Kumar, 2018)

Finally, the third quote is here to remind you how counterproductive it is to worry about the future. Remember, the future isn't set in stone, and you have certain powers to change the outcome if you choose – so why worry?

"Do not ruin today with mourning tomorrow."

~ Catherynne M. Valente (Kumar, 2018)

Distinguishing what you need and what you want

What we need and what we want are two completely different things, often worlds apart. The things you need are a requirement. They are essential, while the things that we want are what we desire or wish for. While we generally understand the difference, our negative distortions can trick us into believing that we need the things we want.

It's a good idea to distinguish between the things you want and need, and you can also prioritize them so that you have complete clarity. To distinguish the difference between your needs and wants, you should consider both your high-level wants and your low-level wants, along with your low-level needs and your high-level needs. Your high-level wants could include your overall career goal, while your low-level wants could be replacing your car within four years. You should:

- Pursue your high-level needs – they are the most important.
- Recognise your low-level needs – they are important too.
- Prioritize your high-level wants – they are your deepest and most-wanted desires.
- Consider your low-level wants – don't pay them too much attention as they should only be considered once you've dealt with your high and low-level needs, and your high-level wants.

Over time, our needs and wants change, so remember they are not static. Simply re-evaluate your needs and wants whenever necessary. However, the way you prioritize your wants and needs always stays the same.

When it comes to the things you need and desire, you must remember that this varies from person to person. It's the personal value we place on things.

Emotional regulation

Emotional regulation helps you filter your emotions, paying attention to the most important pieces of information so that we can deal with them to ensure we are not caused fear or stress. Basically, it helps you to influence the emotions you have, when you have them, and how you experience or express your feelings as a result. It can be an automatic or controlled reaction, and it consists of both positive and negative feelings.

Emotional regulation is helpful for women who suffer from anxiety because it helps to reduce or diminish fear, depending on the emotion. As I mentioned in the introduction, women may find they experience more worry and stress due to the levels of neurotransmitters in the brain. We tend to naturally be more emotional than men (partly because it is more socially acceptable) so managing our emotions is a great skill.

Emotional regulation involves three key components:

1. Inhibiting actions triggered by emotions

2. Modulating responses triggered by emotions

3. Initiating actions triggered by emotions

In an ideal world, the modulating responses triggered by an emotion component is the best way to make the most of the emotional regulation process. Research has found that there is a positive connection between managing depression and anxiety with emotional regulation. It is suggested that women show higher emotional control and social-emotional intelligence when their anxiety levels are lower.

Emotional regulation encourages you to pause between reactions and feelings and slow down before you act. With practice, you then learn to evaluate the situation, rather than acting on impulse. This level of engagement offers value because it encourages you to respond within your core values. Emotional regulation brings self-control, as it allows you to stay calm under pressure which is a powerful thing to do. As you do this, you feel great because you are ultimately protecting your core values and ethics. If you want to use emotional regulation, there are some skills you can use to help you cultivate and sustain this during the most challenging times.

To develop emotional regulation, should practice:

· Self-awareness – this means you notice how you are feeling. You then stop and give yourself some time to explore how you feel. Name specific emotions that you feel. You don't need to do anything else; you simply need to acknowledge the feeling that is pursuing your mind right now.

· Mindfulness – this can help you gain more awareness and explore different aspects of the world. Activities such as sensory relaxation and controlled breathing can calm us down and help us react in a better way.

· Self-compassion – this means setting some time every day to develop your emotional regulation skills. It's important to remind yourself of the positive things in your life, and doing so can change the way we feel and act. You can use daily affirmations, relaxation techniques, meditation, self-care and gratitude journaling as ways to build your self-compassion practice.

· Adaptability – when your emotions are controlling you, you become inflexible and easily distracted. As a result, you may notice that you resist change and find it difficult to cope in certain situations. You can improve your adaptability by evaluating your objectives. Take a moment to work on any goals you have and evaluate them. Break them down into smaller steps if you wish!

· Emotional support – this means you seek emotional support from others. The theory behind this is we can save our own mental energy,

which prevents us from becoming too involved in negativity. If you
need to see a professional or therapist, that's fine, or a close friend
may be willing to help. They can be a solid support for you and can
help you cope with your specific situation. Positive and proactive
communication can help you flourish and make important steps
forward.

· Cognitive reappraisal – this means you alter the way you think.
We've covered this already in previous chapters, when we discussed
role reversal and thought replacements (Chapter 1). Remember, it's
all about perspective, so try to view your cognitions from a different
perspective.

Taking control of your emotions in a calm, efficient way can certainly help you
control and manage your anxiety better. You should try to follow at least some of
these emotional regulation techniques to see which ones work best for you.

There's one thing that anxiety sufferers, in particular, find difficult, and that's
being assertive. In the final part of this chapter, we'll explore some easy ways of
being assertive.

Being assertive

It's challenging to be assertive when you have anxiety issues. People with anxiety,
and women, in particular, aren't always confident, and they worry about the
things they have to (or might have to) face in life. Building assertiveness will help
to build your confidence, allow you to protect your rights, and get what you want.

An assertive woman is able to express her feelings in an effective way. She can
also make clear requests, defend herself, say no, and make her wishes known.
Some women who struggle to be assertive often become overly aggressive, as

although they can express what they want, they do it in such a way that puts their relationships in jeopardy. Other women tend to be completely passive and never get what they want. They are unable to express their wants and needs at all, which causes internal tension and can lead to them being taken advantage of. There are times when these people need extra help with assertiveness, too!

Being assertive serves us well because it improves communication skills and allows us to express how we feel openly. It's a way we can speak up and advocate ourselves.

If you want to be more assertive, you should:

Ø Plan your response in advance – This is useful if you constantly find yourself saying yes to things before you have a chance to reflect. You should have some 'go to' phrases, such as, *'I'll get back to you about that,'* so you're ready to react in the best way, and therefore, you're not caught off-guard.

Ø Don't feel guilty – This is something that happens a lot, especially if you suffer from anxiety. Don't allow the guilt to creep up on you when you assert yourself. It's not personal, and the person you are communicating with should respect that.

Ø Breathe! – If you get nervous when you're trying to be assertive, don't worry; it's a natural feeling. Like anything, practice makes perfect, so the more you practice your assertiveness, the better you will become. Take some time to take deep breaths and calm yourself down. Remind yourself of your intentions and go over your response plan from the first point one more time.

Ø Use positive talk – This may sound strange because firm language is typically used when you're being assertive, but that doesn't mean you shouldn't be positive. When you're positive, you give out a sense of confidence. Use positive self-talk to motivate yourself too, and remind yourself that you're going to do a good job, even if it's a difficult subject, topic or discussion.

Ø Your assertive stance – Body language is vital when you're communicating, as communication isn't simply verbal. The way you stand and conduct yourself can say a lot about you. You can give off a sense of empathy, and you can also show you're a force to be reckoned with. In addition, your body language can give you presence and confidence. It can place you in a strong position, especially if you maintain eye contact.

Ø Self-belief – This is key. So many women don't believe in their own self-worth, but let me say right now, you are worth it! You need to believe in yourself, so ensure you stand up for yourself if anyone treats you disrespectfully.

Ø Boundaries – This is where you draw the line. If you put boundaries in place, it helps you stay in your comfort zone while speaking your mind. Remember, you should stay calm, but ensure your intentions are clear.

Once you've been able to go through your mood journal and identify the different thought patterns you're having, you can use the reframing technique in Chapter 1 and the goal setting and time management techniques in Chapter 2 to set your goals. You can then begin to work on your thinking patterns by following the steps in Chapter 2.

It's time to improve your thinking patterns further, as this will set you on the road to success. Next, we'll focus on the different ways to rebuild your core belief system – you're ready!

Chapter 4

Invalidate - How You Eradicate & Rebuild Your Core Beliefs

We've already explored the basics behind CBT, discussed the best goal setting techniques, and considered our cognitive distortions and negative thinking patterns. However, in order to keep moving forward, we need to go much deeper...

Every negative thought you have is shaped by your core beliefs. Many people don't even realize that they have a core belief system or what their beliefs are, and therefore, they don't realize how ineffective and unrealistic they are. Until you know your core beliefs, you can't hope to change them.

In this chapter, you're going to figure out the core beliefs you hold true. We'll build a better understanding of how they serve us and discuss how to let go or change those that don't. We'll talk about rebuilding beliefs that are more realistic and how we can start to make progress.

Prepare to be both shocked and surprised in this chapter, as we're about to challenge everything you know (or think you know)!

Cognitive restructuring

Cognitive restructuring means discovering your negative thinking patterns and working to change them in the most effective way. We use cognitive restructuring when these thought patterns become so overwhelming and destructive that they start to impact other things in our lives such as our well-being, achievements and relationships.

Cognitive restructuring can help you change your negative thought patterns, and there are many benefits of doing this. It helps you build healthier relationships, replace any unhealthy coping tools or mechanisms, rebuild and develop your confidence and self-esteem, improve your communication skills, and it also lowers your anxiety and stress levels. Although restructuring your cognitive distortions takes time, it's certainly worthwhile, and once this becomes a habit, you'll start to live a happier and healthier life. That's because you will no longer be willing to allow your negative thought patterns to control you!

How to uncover your core beliefs

Your core beliefs are the deeply rooted assumptions you hold about the world, others, and yourself. They are used to shape your thinking and behaviors, and they even shape your reality.

The problem is, our core beliefs are not always accurate or beneficial, and therefore they become the root cause of our problems. They are often responsible for our automatic negative thoughts.

Our core beliefs often stem from childhood. We may change and develop as we get older, but our core beliefs aren't always that flexible, so they become irrelevant and untrue. They constantly try to justify themselves and attempt to make themselves stronger. They hate being challenged, but that's because they've been there for so long and fear change, but change is possible.

Many people have deep-rooted beliefs that suggest they are helpless, unlovable, or worthless. Judith Beck identified these as the three main categories of negative core beliefs about the self (2005, 2011). Often these deep-rooted beliefs are unfounded and unevidenced. Our core beliefs start to develop when we are children, and they are influenced by our family, siblings, teachers and friends. As women, our beliefs about ourselves may be very different to those of men as we receive very diverse messages from the influential people in our lives. For example, if our parents teach us that we should never speak to strangers, they may do this with a loving intention of trying to protect us from harm, and it serves us well for many years. However, as we grow older and become more independent, accessing education, college, moving away from the family home etc, this has to change, or we will forever be wary of unknown people.

Cognitive restructuring means you identify your negative thought patterns, and then you either redirect or interrupt them so that they can't have a self-defeating or destructive impact on you. We've talked already about negative thinking patterns, and we've also discussed some of the most common types of cognitive distortions. This means you are already on the right track when it comes to cognitive restructuring, as you've already started to identify your negative thought patterns.

Here are five key strategies to help you work out your core beliefs and consider how they are affecting you:

1. The first strategy you should use is self-monitoring. If you want to change a thought pattern, you need to be able to identify that it's negative in the first place and recognise the error you're making. As you've already been logging your thoughts as part of your mood journal, you have already begun to partake in self-monitoring. You have shown you can identify the

destructive thought patterns, so now you need to use what you've learned in Chapter 3 and sort your thoughts into the 11 different thinking patterns. This way, when you begin to have negative thoughts, you anticipate them and have the ability to stop them from escalating. This strategy simply involves recognising your thoughts, monitoring them, and identifying which category of negative thought patterns they fall into.

2. The second strategy is using questioning techniques to challenge your assumptions. Challenging yourself is an important part of cognitive restructuring, especially if your assumptions are creating barriers for you. Socratic questioning techniques can be used to assess whether your automatic thoughts are illogical or biased. Socratic questioning is named after Socrates, a Greek philosopher. Basically, this involves asking focused, open-ended questions that encourage you to reflect on the thought itself. You then use that knowledge to utilize different perspectives and identify positive responses and actions. Socratic questioning requires you to be disciplined, and it can take practice. This type of questioning is usually most productive between two people, but you can take some time out and work through the following questions yourself:

- Is my negative thought a fact or an emotion?
- What evidence suggests this is an accurate/inaccurate thought?
- How can I test this belief?
- What is the worst that could happen in light of this thought, and how can I respond to this?
- How else could this information be interpreted?
- Is this really a black-and-white situation, or is it more complex? How is it complex?

Questioning in this way allows you to think of different possibilities that aren't as bad as you may initially think at the instant that the negative thought occurred.

3. The third strategy we'll focus on here is to gather the evidence. If you notice specific negative thought patterns that recur, you should keep track of the activities or events that trigger you. Using your mood journal is a great way to gather your evidence as you can note down your thoughts, but you should also start to log your assumptions and beliefs. Our negative thought patterns are often deeply rooted, but they are often inaccurate and biased too. Replacing them means you need to be able to justify how

irrational they are, and the evidence you collect will allow you to make those judgements. Your questioning techniques can also help you to break them down.

4. What's the alternative? Now, this is a great question that you need to embrace. Restructuring your cognitive distortions means you have to find new ways of looking at something – you have to change your perspective. With that in mind, you need to flip your thoughts and come up with positive, rational explanations to replace your distortions. This isn't an overnight fix, as you've been thinking these thoughts for a long period of time. This has to be practiced time and time again, so that it becomes a habit. You could use affirmations or reflect on your positives – think about the positive relationships you've already built or the positive contributions you've made that strongly indicate that your thoughts are untrue.

5. Assess the advantages and disadvantages of your negative thoughts. You can do this by simply writing down your thought and then by asking yourself what the advantage of this thought is. What are the disadvantages of this thought? For example, if you are embarrassed by something that has happened to you, and are thinking that everyone around you thinks you're an idiot, ask yourself: What are the benefits of 'assuming' that everyone thinks you're an idiot? Does it serve you? What are the disadvantages of this? Consider how it makes you feel! Seeing the pros and cons can help you decide if you need to change this thought pattern, but it also helps you determine the value of each of your thoughts. Is it really worth it?

Ten ways to rebuild your beliefs

Now that you've established how to work out your core beliefs, you need to work on changing them. In order to do that, you should change the way you feel, as this forms the foundation you need to rebuild your beliefs.

You can use the following ten strategies to change how you feel, and in turn, they will help you rebuild your beliefs:

1. Relax – relaxing can help you change how you feel. It can reduce stress and tension, and support you to calm your mind. Relaxing actually helps both your body and mind to rest, and sometimes, it can help you switch off, take time to heal, and then you feel refreshed to deal with a new day. Some women like to relax by taking a hot bubble bath or visiting the spa. Others like to lay down and binge-watch Netflix, while others like to read. Whatever you do to relax, be sure to kick back and enjoy it. Accept that tomorrow is a new day and today is just for you!

2. Be inquisitive – ancient philosophers were so wise because they constantly asked questions. If you want to rebuild your whole belief system, you should be challenging yourself by asking better questions. You should ask questions that empower you, demonstrate you have power in your own life, and direct you to find solutions, as well as ensuring you are open to new possibilities. Don't ask questions like, *Why do I need to do this?* Instead, ask yourself, *How can I make this fun/proactive/effective?*

3. Show your gratitude – this is a simple but effective way to improve how you feel. Appreciate the things you have (like we discussed in earlier chapters), the food you're eating, the life you lead, the job you have, the fact you have a roof over your head, etc. Be thankful for all the things you have that you take for granted – your family, your friends and your home, for instance. Being grateful improves how you feel in general!

4. Don't forget to smile – practicing smiling actually boosts the level of happiness you feel. If you feel flat, smile for thirty seconds and see how it boosts you. If you smile while being grateful, there's an even better outcome. The positivity is flowing!

5. Interrupt your thought patterns – if you find yourself procrastinating or feeling down, it's time to interrupt your thought pattern. To do this, you need to do something unexpected. For example, splash your face with cold water, sing your favorite happy song at the top of your voice, jog on the spot or jump up and down, or even imagine your negative thoughts being repeated in a funny voice – like Mickey Mouse or Scooby-Doo. If you laugh and smile, it breaks the tension, and it often brings you out of your anxiety

or depressive state momentarily, so you have time to collect your thoughts. At this time, you may want to take a short break – make yourself some refreshments before you head back, re-evaluate what you need to do, and start afresh.

6. Have a snack. If your energy levels are running low, have a healthy snack to improve them. Ensure you don't eat too much or too little, as that could make you feel tired and lethargic.

7. Get your boost from an external source – what I mean here is listen or watch someone who inspires you. This could be listening to your favorite song, inspirational speaker, or watching a TV programme or movie that lifts your mood. You could even read a chapter of a book or a blog post by your favorite blogger. The choice is yours, so choose whatever works for you!

8. Create a physical anchor – this is when you choose an emotional state that you want to be able to revert to quickly and on command. It often takes a while to program your mind to use your anchor, so remember to practice and give yourself some time to adjust. Simply stand up, close your eyes and imagine the emotional state that you want to adopt as your anchor. Take a few moments to embrace the feeling and note in your mind exactly how it feels so you can return to this as you need to. Snap your fingers with the hand of your choosing to connect that feeling with the physical act of snapping your fingers. Practice this daily. Once you've made the connection, whenever you feel that you are mentally or physically flagging, take a deep breath, close your eyes, snap your fingers, and revert back to your preferred emotional state.

9. Remember the positive times – it's common to allow ourselves to succumb to negativity, but this can become overwhelming. Negativity only results in bringing you down – there are no benefits. That's why it's important that you recognise when your negativity is on the rise and stop it from escalating. Keep three or four powerful memories and feelings in your reserve, so you can reflect on them when need be. Allow them to wash over you and drown out the negative thoughts. Embrace the positive thoughts and really feel them! Take on the emotions and allow yourself to feel better.

10. Be open to other possibilities that are beneficial to you – this means having faith in yourself, including the way you work, your life,

relationships, money, and exercise. Having faith in yourself can bring the feel-good factor, and it can give you instant gratification. If you do have a problem, remember that there is often more than one answer, and be open to other solutions.

These ten ways can help you rethink and rebuild your whole belief system, allowing you to move forward and improve your life.

What is mental filtering?

We identified mental filtering as a form of negative thinking patterns in Chapter 3. However, just to recap, it's a type of negative thinking that can lead to higher levels of anxiety and depression. Basically, it's when you only see the negatives and overlook the positive or neutral aspects of a situation. If you do this regularly, you really need to reframe or restructure your negative thinking patterns. Expanding on this further, many people want to know how to stop focusing on the negative, which is a really good question...

How you can stop focusing on the negative

If you find that you regularly focus on negative things, there are some things you can do to ensure you take a more positive outlook in life. We've already touched on this throughout all four chapters of this book so far, but just to summarize - if you want to stop focusing on the negatives:

Ø Practice self-awareness and mindfulness.

Ø Go through your mood journal and identify your negative thought patterns to build your awareness.

Ø Replace your negative thoughts with positive feelings and memories (as we discuss earlier in this chapter).

Ø Don't stop your thoughts. Deal with your thoughts and attempt to problem-solve, rather than ignore them.

Ø Cope with criticism. This is something we haven't covered yet, and although, as women, we don't find it easy to accept criticism, the best thing we can do is change the way we view and receive it. Don't see criticism as a critical, personal judgment; simply see it as opinion-based comments that could help you improve or develop. Of course, some criticism is unfounded, but you should plan how to deal with this in advance by preparing some assertive responses – we discussed assertiveness in Chapter 3. Just like your negative thoughts, don't be afraid to ask: where is the evidence? Once you're practiced in not taking criticism personally, you can listen to the feedback you receive and see if you can pull out some developmental points that you can use for the greater good. Practice coping better with the feedback or criticism you receive and accept that everyone is entitled to their own opinion.

Ø There have already been recommendations for having a thought diary, but you can actually incorporate this into your mood journal if need be. If you want to focus specifically on your thinking patterns, you could create a thought diary, and it will help you understand your thoughts, how they cause an emotional response, and the frequency they occur. You can break down the process of your thought in more detail, if you specifically have a diary that focuses solely on them. Alternatively, keep your thoughts as part of your mood journal, but still attempt to examine how they cause your emotional response, their frequency and break them down. Finally, use thought replacement methods discussed in this chapter to overcome them.

Your core beliefs and emotional reasoning

As we work through this chapter together, you'll already be familiar with some of the concepts we're covering, as we've referred to them previously. We've mentioned emotional reasoning, but it's important that we focus on this again in relation to your core beliefs.

It's important to reason with your emotions because sometimes we can't help but feel or think a particular way, even when there's absolutely no reason or evidence for us to feel the way we do. For example, we may feel guilty about doing something for ourselves when there's no logic to feeling this way. This is a type of negative thinking, but it's something that you must challenge. Feelings of guilt are often deeply rooted, so you need to remind yourself why you should not feel guilty. Remember that self-care has benefits as it can improve work ethic, productivity, and relationships, plus keep our stress and anxiety levels low, all of which impact positively on how we perform.

Emotional reasoning is a reflection on your whole belief system as your beliefs are designed on this ability. If you challenge your cognitive distortions by reasoning with your automatic thoughts, you show that you want to seek the truth and are not simply willing to accept the assumptions you make.

We discussed the foundations of emotional reasoning in Chapter 3, but we need to go a little deeper here. Let's remember that our core beliefs are often instilled when we are a child, and therefore emotional reasoning does not demonstrate an informed, adult perspective. If you find that your negative thinking is categorized as emotional reasoning, fortune-telling or mind-reading, then it's likely that your core beliefs are stuck in your unconscious mind and are preventing you from changing.

Be sure to interrogate your thoughts and consider how they impact your belief systems. Only you can reprogramme your mind and change this, over time, through motivation and determination.

Relaxation training

Relaxation is important, especially if you're an anxiety sufferer. Stress and anxiety are on the rise right now, and with them comes fear. Relaxation is an excellent CBT tool to help reduce the stress and anxiety you feel. It's important to recognise that it's actually a short-term coping tool, but it still has its benefits.

Relaxation can help you sleep, reduce stress and worry, and lower your blood pressure. It can even help minimize impulsive behavior too. Research shows that responsiveness is often decreased in those who suffer from higher levels of anxiety. Due to the calming properties involved in relaxation, it can really help you to refocus your mind.

The top five ways to relax if you suffer from anxiety are:
- Try some yoga – yoga regulates your breathing, calms your mind, and encourages your body to stretch. It's a great way to relax and calm your mind and an excellent way to meet new, like-minded women.
- Meditation and mindfulness – meditation and mindfulness can help you create a more positive mindset while also relaxing your mind and body. You can join classes to practise them, or you can easily find videos or audio tracks to follow on the internet.
- Complementary therapies – having a treatment such as a massage, a pedicure, a facial, and forms of reflexology and other alternative therapies are great ways to relax. Treating yourself to an alternative therapy can really help you unwind and feel appreciated.
- Practice regulated breathing – this is similar to yoga and meditation, except it's simply focusing on your breathing. Try a calming technique in which you breathe in for seven seconds, hold for two and breathe out for nine seconds. Breathing out for longer than you breathe in can help you feel calm and relaxed.

· Take a long soak in a warm bath and listen to soothing music if possible – many women find a long soak in the bathtub relaxing, so kick back, unwind, and soak your muscles.

Remember, relaxation is a temporary fix when it comes to anxiety, but a short-lived solution is sometimes what is needed in order to take a moment and regroup. It gives you time to collect your thoughts and rethink your situation. Once you've taken some time to relax, you may realize that things aren't as bad as they seem.

In the next chapter, we're going to focus on staying present. A lot of anxiety occurs because we dwell on the past and worry about the future, so it's time to put a stop to all that unnecessary worry and distress!

Chapter 5

Basic Enlightenment - How You Stay in the Present

Staying present isn't always easy, and what makes it even more complicated is that there are so many misunderstandings about what 'staying present' actually means.

In this chapter, we're going to discuss what is meant by the term 'stay present' and explore how this can lead to a better life and enlighten you. We're also going to look at how we can stay in the present, the drawbacks of worrying about the past, decision making, and fretting about things that haven't happened yet. We will cover mindfulness, and how this can alleviate anxiety, allowing you to comfortably stay in the present, while additionally reviewing some social skills training.

By the end of this chapter, you'll have discovered how staying present can calm your subconscious and help you feel enlightened and empowered so that you can move forward. It's time to remove the worry and fear from your mind.

What does it mean to stay present?

When we talk about staying present, it basically means that you should concentrate on what's happening now rather than dwelling on the past. Sometimes, women focus too much on past experiences or fears, and as a result, we bring that negativity along with us. For example, let's say you have an appointment with the dentist today, but you previously had a bad experience at the dentist, once, several years ago. That dentist has now retired, and yet, every time you visit the dentist, you reflect on your bad experience and bring that negativity along with you. You worry about something similar happening again and end up feeling really worried and anxious before you even get there... Well, there are so many variables involved here and it's highly likely that this bad experience won't happen again, but it's there in your mind, and you're consumed with it.

Staying present can help you avoid this!

Being present can help you lead a happier and healthier life because it encourages you to focus all your energy on the task at hand. By focusing on something specific, you are often more productive and achieve your goals or targets faster. Staying present can also help you take pleasure in the activity you're doing because you're focusing on one thing. Your mind isn't wandering or worrying about the other things you need to do but haven't got around to yet.

Staying present allows you to play an active role in your own life. As a result, many women find that they have a greater connection to those around them and to the actions they take. It gives you a meaning or purpose, which can help you feel fulfilled and happy with your everyday life.

Many people who practice being present feel enlightened as they become aware of their physical and mental needs. Again, this leads to happiness and ensures you stay calm and maintain a rational perspective when dealing with daily life and any issues that occur along the way.

How can we stay present?

When we're enjoying ourselves and having fun, it can be simple to stay in the present, but this feeling isn't permanent. It's all too easy for us to focus on the past or future, which means we don't enjoy the moments we're living.

You must have heard sayings such as 'making the most of it [the situation or event]', and this is a prompt to remind you to stay present and enjoy your life experiences, as you may not get another opportunity. If you focus on future happiness, you may lose sight of what you already have, and you may even downplay certain events without grasping the chance to enjoy them. Taking a moment to enjoy these events and embracing those feelings of happiness or accomplishment is really important.

That sense of gratefulness and gratitude is something everyone should be in touch with because sometimes it's the 'small things' that actually count. They often lay the foundations to a happy, fulfilling and prosperous life. It may be noticing and appreciating the sound of your child laughing as they play, indulging in a comforting hug from your partner after a difficult day, enjoying a coffee and a chat with a friend or snuggling up with your dog on the sofa to watch one of your favorite films.

If you want to stay present, you have to practise. You can do this by:

- **Committing to staying in the present** – when you first begin to remain in the present, it takes effort and commitment. You should start each day by spending some time reminding yourself that you need to make the most of the day ahead and enjoy it, regardless of how things unfold.
- **Creating a routine** – you may find that you have to remind yourself to remain present regularly. To do this, you could set reminders or alarms on your phone to check that you're staying in the present, which helps to build your awareness. You could also set some time aside each day to simply focus on the present

and what it has to offer. The more reverting to the present is practiced, the more likely it is to become a habit so you can live in the present more regularly.

· **Being Aware of your Thoughts** – we've talked about using routine to build your awareness, but you should remain conscious of your thoughts as much as possible. Try to eradicate negative thoughts by replacing them with positive, present-focused thoughts. Try not to worry about the future or the past; just practice shifting your focus back to the current time. Make an extra-special effort to focus on your present situation or concentrate on the activity you're partaking in and try to keep the focus off the future. Simply enjoy the moment and engage in it.

· **Connecting to your body** – being aware of your body is also part of staying in the present. You should be conscious of any needs your body has, such as hunger, physical needs, or pain and deal with them. Being connected and paying attention to your body can help to ensure you stay fit and well. Self-care is a great way to remain present, and it can help you avoid focusing on the future. The more in-tune you are with your body, the healthier and happier you'll be.

· **Knowing what's going on around you** – there's always something going on around us, and often we separate ourselves from this because we're too caught up with what could happen or go on in our own lives. Staying present gives us the opportunity to stop and absorb the things around us that we may often ignore. It helps us to feel grateful and adopt a much more positive mindset. Take some time to notice what's happening. Look around and assimilate your surroundings. Are there any animals, or people, or maybe some stunning views or scenery? Think about anything interesting or beautiful, or pay attention to the movements of the things around you. Most of us make it through the day without paying attention to the world or taking the time to enjoy any of the incredible things it has to offer. Being aware of the things that go on around you can really make you feel appreciative and positive.

· **Experiencing the enjoyment** – how much time do you spend waiting for something? Waiting for the microwave to ping, the kettle to boil, or you can even wait for a taxi or bus. These are

the short-term things we wait for, but sometimes we have to
wait for longer periods of time. Long-term waiting includes
waiting for a milestone birthday or anniversary, waiting for
your holiday, or for a break from work. This is a lot of time
spent waiting for things that are in the not-so-near future. The
problem with waiting is that you know you're doing it.
Sometimes, you may see this as wasting time and become
impatient, but what if you flipped this idea and tried not to
think of yourself as 'waiting'? Let's say you're queuing for the
cash machine, and rather than seeing this as 'waiting in the
queue,' you decide that you're going to take in the fresh air and
enjoy your time outside, watching your surroundings. Once you
take your turn at the cash machine, you can carry on with your
day, but in the meantime, you have the opportunity to turn that
'waiting' time into a pleasant, engaging time. Altering your
perspective on the whole idea of waiting can encourage you to
be calmer, patient, and it means you are less frustrated. This is
a great way to live in the present, but it's your choice to change
your perspective on how you view such things.

Stop worrying about the past

We are all capable of worrying, but do you ever wonder... What's the point?
Worrying often becomes a habit, but there's no value in this. It's useless and
pointless because worrying changes nothing. Take a look at the quote below by
John Lubbock:

"A day of worry is more exhausting than a week of work."

~ John Lubbock (Brainy Quotes)

He makes a great point here... Worrying *is* exhausting! It doesn't prevent
something negative from happening, but the worry tires you out and prevents you
from enjoying the positive.

Worrying is a habit that we sometimes develop, and yet it does not serve us with any value. It's a destructive tendency that only causes us to be upset. Even though worrying serves no purpose, so many women find themselves entangled in a cycle of worry. Too much worrying can cause stress and anxiety; it can impact your circulation, which impacts your heart and your whole nervous system.

If you find that you worry a lot about things that have happened in the past, you need to remember you can change this. Worrying is a mindset, and you can alter this. When you're worrying about past events, it's pointless because you can't change the past and the likelihood of experiencing the same thing again is, in most cases, very unlikely.

To deal with your past worries and remain in the present, you have to put things into perspective. There are two ways to do this:

1. Review the situation in an honest way and consider the worst-case scenario. What's the worst that could happen? Often this isn't as bad as we first imagine.

2. Mentally prepare yourself for this, just in case you have to deal with it. Preparation is key – it's unlikely that the worst will occur, but if we're prepared for the worst, anything else will be an improvement.

Worrying about the past does not alter what happens today. You are the only person who can make the change by making a conscious decision not to focus on the things we can't modify. The key is to try and adjust your mindset in relation to worry, so if you find yourself stuck in that worrying habit, bring yourself back into the present and think about all the things you are grateful for. Smile as you visualize these things!

Decision making

Decision making can become an issue if you don't fully believe in your ability to make choices. It can be difficult to think rationally when you are filled with worry. As we've already discovered, staying in the present encourages a more positive and focused mindset, and therefore, a better decision-making capacity.

If we doubt our decision making and ask others for their advice, we risk giving them control when we should be aiming to make better decisions for ourselves. As focusing on the present allows us to concentrate and think clearly, you can learn to trust your own instincts and build your confidence when it comes to decision making.

Indecisiveness often holds us back as it imposes limits on us when it comes to future opportunities. You can enhance your life if you kick the indecisiveness habit. You can do this by:

1. Don't overthink the outcomes of a decision. The truth is, we don't always know the outcomes, and we certainly can't always control them. The things that happen in our lives are not predictable, so overthinking is a waste of time. Make an informed decision and stick to it.

2. Making decisions can sometimes be a little scary, but that's because decision making often comes with risk. There wouldn't be any decisions to make if there was no risk, but sometimes we fear failure. Have faith in your decision choices, and don't be afraid to choose the option that scares you the most.

3. Never make an impulsive decision. The most important thing to do when making a decision is to ensure you are being rational. While decision making can be challenging, it's essential to go through the entire process – think it out and weigh up the pros and cons.

4. Listen to your head and your heart. When decision-making, you need to try and follow both your mind and your instincts. Therefore, you have to find the right balance between the two. While going with your mind is likely to lead you to the safest decision, this isn't always for the best. Going with your instincts is often too impulsive if you don't think about it thoroughly enough.

5. Although it's important to stay present, it's also essential that we learn from our previous experiences. It's okay to briefly reflect on a good decision you've made, to remind yourself that you're capable of making positive decisions. This will help you instill confidence in your own decision making. However, remember to keep centered by bringing yourself back to the present to weigh up the pros and cons.

Worrying about things that haven't happened

Anticipatory anxiety is the anxiety we feel about bad things that haven't happened yet but could possibly happen. This commonly focuses on those things that we can't control or predict and includes the fear and worry we feel as a result. For some women, anticipatory anxiety has side effects, such as not being able to sleep due to excessive worrying. In order to overcome this, you should bring yourself back to the present, so you can assess the situation and put things into perspective.

According to Sara Lindberg (2018), 40 million Americans live with anxiety and have been told by people they love that they 'worry too much.' If you are a mother with teenagers, you have probably heard this phrase a thousand times! As women, we have a tendency to worry about everyone, whether that's our partner, parents, children, friends, animals, neighbors, etc. When we worry, our anxiety is heightened, but anxious people also tend to worry more. Although worry and anxiety are linked, they are not the same thing, and yet they both work hand in hand, which can make our lives more difficult.

People who suffer from anticipatory anxiety often think the worst-case scenario is ALWAYS going to happen. They report symptoms such as:

· Lack of concentration
· Inability to manage mood and emotions
· Tense muscles or muscle pain
· Sleep issues
· Restlessness and unease
· Numbness when it comes to emotions
· Appetite loss and nausea

The best way to cope with this type of worry is to ensure you have enough sleep, exercise well and eat a healthy diet to guarantee you get all the nutrients your body needs. Of course, your anxiety will try to persuade you otherwise, but even just eating small meals will help. In addition, you should cut back on caffeine, and if you try relaxation techniques before bed, you may find it improves your sleep.

The most important point when it comes to dealing with worrying is to ground yourself. Reconnect yourself to the present by focusing on a task or using physical items such as snapping a band against your wrist.

Improving your anxiety with mindfulness

Mindfulness is a practice based on our ability to be aware of where we are and what we're doing, while remaining fully present. It encourages us to deal with the situations we face while not overreacting or feeling overwhelmed by them or life in general.

Mindfulness has many benefits. It is a great way to improve your anxiety, and it is a great way to help you reconnect with the present. Practicing mindfulness can:
- Reduce stress
- Help us gain insight into our own mind
- Increase our attention
- Enhance performance
- Prevent us from making unfounded judgements

Mindfulness is a practice that many people do because they feel it enriches their lives. It helps you relax and calm your mind, but it can also inspire you and spark innovation.

Mindfulness helps you to cultivate a positive mindset. You can practice mindfulness by:

Ø Walking, sitting, standing and moving. You can also lay down, but this can encourage you to fall asleep.

Ø Merging it with meditation practices such as yoga.

Ø Taking short pauses throughout the day.

The practice itself is simple. Simply clear your mind and concentrate on what you are doing or what's happening to you. It will help you work through your fear and anxiety, so that you can remove it from your mind. Think about all of your senses and focus on your body. What sounds can you hear close to you and further away? Can you hear the sound of your breathing? What can you feel? Can you feel the touch of your clothes on your skin, the wind on your face or the connection of your body with where you are sitting? Can you taste or smell anything? What can you see? Pay attention to the color, textures and beauty that surrounds you. Even if you only do this for a few minutes, you will feel much calmer and able to continue with your day.

Mindfulness helps you focus on yourself for a change.

Social Skills Training

Social interactions are not always easy for women with anxiety. CBT can help you build and strengthen your social skills so that you can communicate effectively. Social skills training in CBT is tailored for you as an individual.

In order to improve your social skills, you first have to assess them. To do this, you should ask yourself:

1. What social interactions are more challenging for me?

2. What social skills or interactions could I improve?

This can then help you identify your specific social skills training targets as you base them on the things you find most difficult.

Social Skills Training Techniques include:

· Corrective feedback – you can use feedback to help improve your
social skills. This entails you carrying out a social interaction
and another person commenting on how you can improve this.

· Positive reinforcement – you can use rewards when improvements
are made in social interactions or skills. The reward can be
anything you choose that will motivate you.

· Behavioral rehearsal – this means that you partake in roleplay,
practicing your new social skills with another person or during a
therapy session.

· Instruction – this is more of an educational part of social skills
training which involves modeling specific behaviors.

· Weekly homework – your therapist can set goals for you to practice
your social skills, or you can set your own targets so that you
can practice your social skills in more challenging situations.

Social skills training is all about interactions and communication. Here are my
top five tips on how you can communicate with others better, as practice makes
perfect:

- Assertiveness is a key part of improving your social skills, and we have
already covered this in a previous chapter.

- Use non-verbal communication such as body language and signals.

- Introduce yourself or your conversation. This helps to set others at ease
as you're telling them what you want to discuss with them.

- Listening actively includes asking questions, reflecting on what has been
said, and paying attention to others.

- Be willing to accept and give compliments. Sometimes, people don't take
or give compliments easily, but this can actually be a great way to start a
conversation.

Throughout Chapter 5, we've focused on the idea of staying present, explored
how this leads to a better life and also, how it can enlighten you. We've examined
the benefits and drawbacks an anxiety sufferer may experience when they are
starting to practise staying in the present, and we've discussed the best way for

you to progress when it comes to this. Before you move on to the next chapter, take some time to practise mindfulness and also practise staying present.

You never know, you may start to enjoy it. Next, we'll begin to consider how we can move forward.

Tomorrow is a new day!

Chapter 6

Idling - How You Move Forward and Just Get Started

You're now more than halfway through The VISIBILITY Method, and it's understandable that you may feel some reluctance while on your journey. Lack of self-belief can be a driving factor, and this chapter focuses on the reluctance you might feel so far and will get you back on track. If you lack belief in yourself right now, although this isn't going to change overnight, I know you can do this.

You've made it!

Before you go any further, it's important that you celebrate your success so far. This is something that many women don't do, but only picking up on the negatives can be soul-destroying. You probably recognise the pattern - you compliment a friend on what she is wearing, and she says, 'Oh, this old thing? I've had it for years - I should probably stop wearing it. And don't look at my hair - I've got an appointment to get it cut next week...' Or maybe this would be your response! This is another example of how your thought patterns need to be altered, so repeat after me...

"It's okay to celebrate my own successes and achievements."

It seems human nature to only point out the negatives, but most women need to hear that they are doing something well too. We need to champion ourselves and each other! The next time you find yourself picking out the negatives, match them with a positive. So, if you're not happy with something later today or tomorrow, make a conscious effort to point out something you've recently done well or are happy with.

It will help you make a positive start to your day, and then you'll feel ready to challenge a 'can't do' attitude.

A 'can't do' attitude

A 'can't do' attitude is a defeatist attitude that you allow into your head, as you believe you can't do something without even attempting to do it. Have you ever heard or used phrases such as... *"This can't be done!"* <u>OR</u> *"I can't do that/it!"*

Would it surprise you to know that most of the things we say can't be done can be done? It's simply your 'can't do' attitude that has persuaded you of this, and rather than thinking logically and problem-solving the situation, we accept this untrue belief. Take a few minutes to reflect - I imagine there are lots of things in your life that you are doing and have achieved right now that you initially thought were impossible. Whenever you want to quit or not even attempt something, think of Thomas Edison. It took him over 10,000 attempts before he successfully created the lightbulb. Thank goodness he didn't give up!

These defeatist thought patterns become second nature, and we often don't bother to question them. We should be investigating them, challenging them, and writing ourselves a new habit. There are three simple yet powerful ways to combat a 'can't do' attitude and change the pattern. In order to do this, you should develop your 'can do' attitude:

> 1. Focus on your value. Self-worth is so crucial as you control the value you place on yourself. Having a 'can do' attitude means you believe in yourself, and that's so important if you want to succeed!

> 2. Don't play the blame game! A woman who has a 'can do' attitude focuses on the present and solutions; she doesn't blame herself or anyone else because everything can be remedied.

3. Learn from your mistakes and move on. Don't become obsessed with past mistakes. We all make mistakes, but the best way to move on and grow is by learning from them. How you handle mistakes impacts your future performance, so use them as a learning curve – it's for the greater good!

4. Don't compare yourself to others. You should only ever measure yourself against personal targets – try to improve yourself and strive towards your own goals. Measuring yourself against your personal goals can really help you maintain focus.

5. Don't miss opportunities that present themselves to you. Pay attention to what goes on around you and read up on things that mean something. Keep on educating yourself by learning new things whenever you find the time. Knowledge is power!

6. Talk about it! Don't allow things to get on top of you and drag you down. If there's someone you can talk things over with, do it. Sharing the ups and downs with someone you trust can really help you deal with the things that bother you and move on. Talking can help you maintain a positive outlook and your 'can do' attitude.

7. Practice gratitude and focus your energy on the positive. We've discussed this already, but it is extremely important if you want to ensure that you maintain a 'can do' attitude.

Eradicating your 'can't do' attitude and replacing it with a 'can do' one takes some work, but it leads to a happier, healthier life with improved wellbeing. When you have the right attitude, good things happen. You don't get bogged down with all the stresses and strains of life, and it truly makes a difference to how you feel.

What is reluctance, and why do we feel reluctant?

Reluctance occurs when we genuinely don't want to do something, and we try to avoid having to do it. If we have to complete a task that we don't really want to do, we may not do it well because of the reluctance we feel.

The reason we're discussing reluctance right now is that, at this stage, you may be feeling reluctant to continue with the work you've been putting into working on your anxiety. It's important to remember you're at a critical stage of your development as we're trying to create positive habits, so it's essential you don't let them slide.

There's no doubt, your motivation will be tested, but if you fully commit and invest yourself, I know you can succeed. Let's recap some of the most important things we've learned so far.

Recap – The Core Concepts

It's necessary to regroup at this point and reflect on the things we've already covered in this book so far. Below, we'll briefly reflect on each chapter to remind us of the core concepts we should be following.

In Chapter 1, we began our CBT journey as we talked through the basics, plus how to identify cognitive distortions and negative thought patterns.

1. Do you still check in with yourself?

2. Have you been writing down your negative thoughts?

3. Have you tried the opposite threes technique?

In Chapter 2, we talked about personal goal setting and reflected on how we can create a personalized routine that suits us. We also explored overthinking and how this can increase our anxiety levels before discussing organizational techniques that alleviate stress, such as time management.

1. Have you set some personal SMART goals and objectives?

2. Have you tried journaling, and have you challenged your thoughts?

3. Have you noticed any positive changes in relation to your anxiety?

In Chapter 3, we shifted the focus onto harmful or negative thoughts, and we considered how we could pinpoint and cope with each of these. We explored the 11 different thinking patterns and discussed the things we can and can't control.

1. Did you create your own stress management plan?

2. Have you practiced gratitude by focusing on what you can do, or what you have, rather than the things you don't?

3. Can you distinguish between your needs and wants?

4. Have you been practicing assertiveness?

In Chapter 4, we talked about destroying your negative beliefs and rebuilding new, positive core beliefs. This takes time and is not something that can be mastered quickly.

1. Are you able to recognise and acknowledge your core beliefs?

2. Have you been able to analyze them and rebuild your new core beliefs based on what you've learned?

3. Have you been working through the ten ways to rebuild your belief system?

4. Have you built relaxation techniques into your routine?

In Chapter 5, we focused on staying present and stopping worrying about the past or things that haven't happened yet.

1. Do you have your indecisiveness under control when it comes to decision making?

2. Are you fully committed to staying present and have you been practicing this?

3. Does mindfulness help with your anxiety?

4. Have you been challenging your social skills?

The five chapters we've recapped here are laying the foundations of The VISIBILITY Method. Once you have the basics in place, it's time to move onto the growth stage – because you can make further improvements to your life.

Anxiety is a key focus throughout this book, so now it's time to discuss the best ways to combat it.

The Best Ways to Combat Anxiety

When anxiety kicks in, we automatically go into fight-or-flight mode, as our brain is warning us of impending danger, and we need to act quickly to keep ourselves safe. Women who suffer from anxiety become uncomfortable because it isn't a pleasant feeling. However, avoiding it can escalate the issue and make your short-term anxiety become a long-term problem.

Many women wonder what the best way to combat anxiety is, and the simple answer is 'nothing.' This isn't a negative response; it's a way to calm your mind so that you can deal with it rationally. The thing with anxiety is it allows us to blow things out of proportion. If we stop attending to the issue, our brain assumes the situation is no longer a danger, so there is no need to dramatize the event. The brain also learns that similar experiences do not need so much immediate attention in the future.

You should give this a try next time something happens that makes you feel anxious. Simply acknowledge it but shift your attention swiftly back to the present. Once you're calm, you can assess if you need to respond to the situation, or you may decide it wasn't that important in the first place.

The P-Word

Do you know what the dreaded 'P' word is?

Let me just add; we don't have to feel a sense of dread when we hear the word procrastination. You see, we are all capable of procrastinating; in fact, it's really common because it's our mind's way of dealing with the tasks we don't want to do.

Procrastinating means that you subconsciously avoid a specific task because you don't want to do it. Maybe the chore is difficult, boring, stressful, unenjoyable, or simply just unpleasant, and you don't feel motivated to do it. Whatever the reason, it triggers a sense of anxiety and overwhelms us, which prevents us from completing the task.

Many people believe that low self-esteem is a reason behind procrastination, but perfectionism is also a lead cause. This is because we may feel we're not up to the task or can't complete it as well as someone else, and nothing other than perfect is acceptable. If we're not feeling up to it, it's easier to ignore it and say we'll do that 'later.' That's because the more we procrastinate, the more we feel like a failure for not carrying out the chore. Even though we're trying to ignore the task and keep pretending that it isn't important, we know in our head that it is. Therefore, part of our mind is stressing about the fact we haven't done it yet.

Some women are well aware that they are master procrastinators, while others don't even know they do this. Let's look at some of the key signs that indicate we are procrastinating...

How to identify and overcome procrastination

If you're not productive, then it's likely you're procrastinating. Procrastination is the polar opposite of productiveness. People who are productive get things done, are motivated, have clear goals and clarity, overcome any barriers that stand in their way, and are not afraid of failure. They are focused, and therefore produce a high standard of work at a fast pace.

As women, particularly mothers, it may be that you are really organized and productive when it comes to things like sorting the kids out for school. However, perhaps you procrastinate when the house is empty, and you can turn your attention to yourself.

Here are some of the key indicators that suggest you are procrastinating:
- You make excuses to explain why you've not completed the task you need to complete.
- You do not have uncertain or unrealistic goals.
- You are unable to concentrate.
- Failure bothers you.
- You feel overwhelmed every time you think of a specific task.
- The task bores you.
- You are holding onto negative beliefs and believe you can't complete the task well before you've even tried.

If you experience any of these things, then you need to take action. You need to overcome your procrastination before it takes hold and battles with your anxiety.

To overcome procrastination, you may want to:
- Identify your fears and work out how you'll overcome them.
- Focus on progress rather than perfection.

- Set clear goals and break them down into smaller
  chunks so that you can track your achievements.
- Adopt a positive, can-do attitude.
- Try to work away from distractions and discipline
  yourself to ensure you spend time focusing.
- Make a to-do list and prioritize your tasks so you have
  something to work from.
- Reward yourself for your achievements.
- Practice mindfulness and relaxation to prepare you for
  the hard work ahead.

The key to preventing procrastination is organizing your time effectively and being able to stay focused on your tasks. You could try time blocking to keep you motivated and on target.

CBT for Emotional Regulation

We mentioned emotional regulation in previous chapters, but before we move on to the next chapter, it's important to review this. To summarize, emotional regulation is when we can control our emotions, which helps us cope better with certain situations.

You may remember that regulating emotions is broken down into three key areas:
-

1. Reducing emotional triggers – when an experience triggers negative emotions.

2. Reducing emotional intensity – when the triggered emotion is maintained at a manageable level, without intensifying to an overwhelming level.

3. Reducing the duration of emotion – when you work to bring it back down to its normal level, following the peak of emotion.

There are many events that can lead to the heightening of your emotions, which causes dysregulation. Typically, we learn to regulate our feelings as we go from childhood to adulthood, but if the development of emotions is disturbed, it can result in persistent dysfunctions. In women, this usually occurs as a result of trauma, sensitivity (because some people are much more sensitive than others) or due to growing up in an invalidating environment. This means that you have learned to distrust or ignore others and their emotional cues. As a result, you may struggle to engage when you or the people around you are suffering from intense emotions.

There are a number of CBT treatments available for emotion regulation. These include mindfulness, training in emotional regulation, interpersonal effectiveness and distress tolerance. We've covered mindfulness and emotion regulation training already, and each of these can be an effective treatment.

Distress tolerance refers to the ability to accept your emotions, work with unpleasant emotions or urges, and avoid them because you're not ready to deal with them. Interpersonal effectiveness includes emotion regulation, but when you suffer from the intense emotion, you make changes to your environment to prevent it from happening again.

Episodes of anxiety, extreme emotion and procrastination commonly link to the fear we feel. That's why, in Chapter 7, we'll be looking at how you can remove your worry and fear.

Chapter 7

Let go - How You Really Let Go and Remove Worry and Fear from Your Mind

In Chapter 7, we're turning our focus to the growth stage of your development. Sometimes, we have to be brave and let go, pushing through the fear and worry. Working through such anxieties isn't easy, but it's something you can train yourself to do.

Sometimes, worry is uncontrollable, and it's essential to understand why we worry in the first place. We need to overcome our fears by figuring out solutions in a rational way that continues to serve us best. It's natural to experience worry from time to time, so it's important to remember that everyone has feelings such as this.

Worries and fears are also common when we have to make decisions in our lives because our mind views them as a risk. Having to make a choice weighs heavily on our shoulders and is why we experience worry, anxiety and fear. We have to accept that while some decisions are good, others are bad, but our decisions do not define us as women.

Why do we worry?

The act of worrying is an unconscious action. It happens because we think about the future and imagine things aren't going to end well – which makes us feel fear. It's an automatic reaction, but some key reasons why we worry are because:

1. We are uncertain about the future - whether that is our future or someone we care about, such as our family or friends.

2. It gives our mind something to focus on while waiting for an event to happen.

3. We are unable to take direct action, so we allow ourselves to worry because that's what we do.

4. Our mind never relaxes or rests, so worrying becomes a natural reaction when we are unable to do anything about a particular situation.

Worrying can have its own side effects, too. It encourages us to adopt a more negative mindset, which can increase anxiety, worry and amplify destructive thought patterns. Obsessive worrying brings on stress, especially if you allow it to become a habit. We can also be harmed in other ways, as it can lead to heart problems and nervous disorders along with stomach issues such as indigestion and constipation, plus headaches and tiredness. Excessive worrying can also cause sleeplessness, lack of concentration, and struggles with clarity as we cannot think straight.

There are some things you can do if you find yourself excessively worrying. They include:
- Remember that you can never really foresee the future, so stop trying to control your destiny beyond your ability. Just make some plans to overcome the things that worry you.
- Try to gain a deeper understanding of the mind and remember, you are in control. If you're keeping a mood journal, as advised in Chapter 1, you can monitor your thoughts and understand why you're feeling the way you do.
- Live in the present moment, not the future, just like we talked about in Chapter 5. There are so many benefits in doing so, and this includes reducing your excessive worrying.

Worrying prevents us from making important decisions, and it often means we lose control of our thoughts. Frequently, things happen because they are meant to happen, so being frightened of what 'could' occur serves no purpose or value.

How to Crush Intrusive Thoughts

While we can all experience thoughts that are intrusive, we don't always realize that they are actually happening. Some of our negative thoughts are uncomfortable to deal with, and managing such problems can be difficult. Intrusive thoughts are unwanted thoughts or images that pop into our minds and cause us to be distressed. These thoughts escalate the fears you feel and can result in additional inappropriate or disturbing thoughts. It's time to take action, preferably before they become obsessive.

You can crush intrusive thoughts in the following ways:

- Understand your thoughts and discover the reason they're happening by questioning 'why' you're thinking that way. Also, reflect on your core values.
- Make sure you don't ignore the thought, as it's important to deal with it.
- Don't fear how you think or feel. Assess your thoughts and emotions to see how rational they are. Consider how they are affecting you - are they dangerous?
- Don't take it personally! Our thoughts are not 'real' - they are our opinions or judgements, which are not always based on facts or evidence. Reason with yourself and build your sense of trust in yourself.
- Don't change your behaviours due to your thoughts. Acting irrationally can be a common reaction when you're having intrusive thoughts, and it can result in compulsive behaviors, but this is not a solution. You could alter your actions negatively; for example, you could avoid going to certain places because of your thoughts, but does this mean you'll never go to another party?

If you suffer significantly from intrusive thoughts, you may benefit from receiving professional help from a medical professional, so don't be afraid to get support and advice if you need it.

All or nothing thinking

We've already discussed all or nothing thinking, but it's important to touch on this again as it is the most common form. It becomes a problem when we're making important decisions, as it means we think in extremes – it's either success or failure, with nothing in between. Often, this is not an effective point of view.

Thinking in an all or nothing way limits our ability to think rationally, as things are not always that simple. It would be narrow-minded to think that our thoughts are linear, as things are often more complicated or complex. Take a moment and recall a 'problematic' thought that you've experienced and consider the different ways to resolve it. You see, there is always more than one path to solving a problem, and while you may choose one particular route, someone else may take another. They could both lead to the same, or different destinations, but regardless, all or nothing thinking does not work well. Sometimes we need to come up with a longer-term plan or a temporary solution.

In order to deal with these thoughts and overcome this issue, you have to restructure the way you think. The best way to describe this is to look at your thinking through different coloured lenses, so you get different perspectives. You should consider your thoughts and challenge them by asking yourself the following questions:

      · What exactly does it mean (is it a problem)? How does it make you feel?

· How might another person view this problem (put yourself in someone else's shoes)?

· What's the best possible outcome or end goal in relation to this (how do you want things to be)?

· How can you get to the best possible outcome (think of the steps along the way)?

· Are there any variables to consider? For example, think about the flexibility you have when resolving the problem, or the barriers you may encounter along the way.

By challenging your thoughts, you start altering the way you think, and your mind begins to learn and think in a much more rounded way, rather than linear. When you think in this way, you start to adopt a much more optimistic mindset, especially if you feel like you've achieved something or have made progress.

Fighting your fears

Fear and anxiety often impact our decision-making skills but not in a way that serves us best. We've spoken a lot about thinking rationally, but when fear and anxiety take hold, it's impossible to think in such a way. Coping with these issues day-to-day is not always easy to deal with, but there are some ways in which you can fight your fears:

· Breathe through the panic

Many people report a faster heartbeat when they are panicking, while others say they have sweaty palms. Although you can't exactly fight your way through the panic, you can take action to calm your mind by simply breathing. Try to use your mind to cope with the panic you're feeling. Simply close your eyes, place your palm on your stomach and breathe deeply but slowly.

· Take some time

It's important that you take some time to think clearly when you are fighting your fears. You have to calm yourself down and distract yourself. You could do this by simply reading a book, having a bath, making a coffee, or taking a short walk.

· What's the worst-case scenario?

Think about the worst possible outcome that can happen and imagine it. Sometimes the worst thing isn't as bad as we anticipate, and we can consider how we would deal with it. Remember that thinking about a particular situation doesn't make it happen, and after doing this, you may realize that your fear is highly unlikely.

· Face your fears

Avoiding our fears only makes things worse, as it makes them more intimidating. When we face our fears, we feel empowered, and the fear itself starts to fade. This is how we can overcome and eradicate fears so that they no longer bother us.

· Don't worry about perfection

There's a saying: 'done is better than perfect,' and while some people will argue this isn't true, sometimes the idea of perfection sets us up to fail. You see, perfection means that there are no flaws or imperfections in something, which is rarely possible. Regardless of what you believe, you shouldn't try to be perfect; you should be more realistic and flexible! Life is all about living, and setbacks happen. You can't let that deter you from striving for and achieving your goals, but you do need to accept that the best solution to your problem may not always be the most perfect.

· Let's talk

Talking can be a kind of therapy, so sharing your thoughts and fears can sometimes feel overwhelming but also freeing. If you can't talk to your friends or family, there are helplines that may be useful for you. You can also speak to your GP.

· The basics

Sometimes, you have to go back to basics. Many women turn to other things like alcohol or drugs to help with their anxiety, but this only makes things worse in the long term. It's the simple things that can make all the difference when it comes to anxiety, such as a healthy meal, a good night's rest, self-care, and light exercise such as a walk.

· Where's the evidence?

When you are fighting your fears, you need to overcome a lot, so it's important to look at the evidence available. This helps you to challenge thoughts and consider your situation from a different

perspective. What would you tell a friend or family member if they
had a similar fear to you right now?

· Think of your happy place

Everyone has a happy place; you just have to visualize it! Close your
eyes and take a moment to imagine your favorite soothing place. This
should be a place you feel safe. Soak in your memories and let your
positive feelings flow.

· What about a reward?

Many people find it motivational to reward themselves for
overcoming their fears. So, if you do something that you've been
dreading, treat yourself and do something that makes you happy.

Problem-solving therapy

Problem-solving therapy is an action-orientated type of talking therapy that
focuses on problems in detail. The approach itself provides insight based on our
past experiences, and yet, it also allows you to focus on the present, and make
permanent rather than temporary changes.

Problem-solving therapy helps you cope with any barriers or challenges that
stand in your way, and it encourages you to resolve your problems. By doing this,
you can reduce negative emotions, improve relationships, and achieve your long
and short-term goals. You can gain control and play an active role in the
decisions that you need to make.

This treatment focuses on specific problems and encourages you to address them.
As you do this independently, it creates a sense of interest and confidence in your
life. Problem-solving therapy includes:

· Addressing problems directly by breaking down the problem.

· Defining your problems by focusing on what the problem is and
what is the root cause.

· Brainstorming and evaluating problem-solving techniques. These
allow you to assess the effectiveness of multiple solutions to the

things causing you distress in your life by breaking them down into easy steps. You can set goals here and monitor your progress.

· Act by taking some kind of action, even if the problem can't be broken down. This can help reduce feeling overwhelmed and allow you to produce a clear plan of action so that you can achieve your goals.

Removing worry and fear from your mind takes time. It's not a quick fix, especially when making tough decisions that you know are going to affect you and your family. When you have to make decisions, you need to feel a strong sense of acceptance, because there are difficult choices to be made, there are ones that have no 'great' solutions, and there are times when we make the wrong decisions. In truth, we never really know how any of the decisions we make are going to work out for certain, and that's why it's important to weigh up the pros and cons. The way you handle problems does not define you as a mother, wife, daughter, friend or woman. You can always go back and revise your decisions later.

The best advice to take on board here is to make the best choice you can, to the best of your ability. The more well-informed decisions you make, the more confident you become, and the more comfortable you will be in the whole decision-making process. Next, let's move on and discuss how you can deal with and release any pent up anger you feel.

Chapter 8

Instruct - How to Tell Your Mind to Release the Pent Up Anger Inside You

Anger is simply a strong feeling of hostility or displeasure, and it's something that we all feel from time to time. Sometimes, it's a reaction that we can't always control well. Some of us let it out instantly, while others bottle it up until it spills over or erupts aggressively. To feel anger is upsetting, but many women experience additional emotions following an angry outburst. The truth is, unless we deal with our anger effectively, it can end up controlling or consuming us.

In this short chapter, we'll learn more about anger and how to deal with angry thoughts. We will explore how you can deal with your rage and consider how it links to anxiety. We will also explore anger management therapy, so you can manage anger - especially the pent-up feelings that you sometimes have inside.

Before we delve deeper, it's important to begin to understand more about anger.

What is anger?

The most important thing to remember about anger is that it's a normal, healthy emotion. Many people believe it's a 'bad' emotion, but this is a misconception as there are positives to it. Everyone experiences this emotion at some stage. As women, we may feel anger if we're frustrated, deceived or attacked. We can also feel anger if we feel invalidated or that we've been treated unfairly. Anger can motivate us and encourage change, it can help us identify problems and issues, and it can also help us stay safe or stick up for ourselves if need be.

As anger tends to come across in displays of aggression, it is considered more of a masculine than feminine trait, and it can be perceived very differently by society. In men, anger can make them be seen as powerful, in control, dominant, self-assured, whereas in women, they are considered difficult and shrill. As children, we are often conditioned to be quiet and submissive, compared to our brothers and male cousins, who are actively encouraged to stand up for themselves.

Within politics, for example, according to author Rebecca Traister, anger and determination can be a reason why people vote for men but are cited as reasons not to vote for a woman. She says, "Society shuns angry women, convincing them that their rage is impolite, unattractive, or even unhealthy." This disparity is interesting as we all have the right to experience anger when someone treats us unfairly, and anger can facilitate powerful change when channeled in the right way.

However, anger sometimes gets out of hand, and it can harm others, including yourself. If you struggle to express your anger or express it in an unhelpful way, it can become problematic as you're not in control. Anger can have a negative impact on both our physical and mental health, which often results in more feelings of anger.

As with all our emotions, anger causes us to react, but when our anger is out of control, our behavior is unhelpful. For example, rage can cause outward aggression, violence or passive aggression, which basically means turning a blind eye and ignoring the issues, or inward aggression, where you hate yourself and sometimes even deny yourself of your basic needs. Such responses indicate that your anger is no longer healthy; in fact, it's out of control.

Why is pent-up anger so dangerous?

Women with pent-up anger often respond in destructive ways as they feel
resentment towards themselves or feelings of unworthiness. Pent-up rage means
that you've been bottling up your feelings rather than expressing and dealing with
them. This causes your feelings to erupt uncontrollably because there's no other
way to cope with them and they need to be released. You've probably heard
sayings such as 'flipped out' or 'lost it' when people lose their temper or express
their anger in an aggressive way, but it's so dangerous because they are not in
control. If you are unable to cope effectively, anger can end up controlling your
life.

Pent-up anger can cause many health issues. It can affect your nervous system,
increase your blood pressure and your heart rate too. It can cause a lot of stress,
and it can also lead to anxiety if symptoms escalate. Let's talk about this in more
detail.

How are anger and anxiety linked?

There are many commonalities between anxiety and anger, and yet they are often
overlooked. We've talked about anxiety a lot throughout this book so far, and it's
important to remember that anxiety is closely linked to worry and fear, just like
anger. Anger causes further stress, yet, anxiety is caused by overstimulation,
often from stressful situations. Looking at this from another perspective, anxiety,
if left unchecked, can also lead to feelings of anger. If a person is worried or
scared about something, anger can present to mask anxiety, when it's the feelings
of anxiety that are stirring up the frustration and anger inside.

When you feel extremely angry, you could experience the following symptoms:

- · Clammy hands
- · Shortness of breath
- · Racing heartbeat
- · Lashing out

If you give in to these feelings, you could find yourself partaking in risky behaviors. For example, you could make rash decisions, and it could also ruin your relationships with friends and loved ones. Anger is not always linked to anxiety, so it's important to assess why you're feeling the way you do. Exploring your anger triggers is a great way to start thinking about the cause of your anger, which helps you work out a positive response because it becomes overpowering. For example, a person who suffers from sleep deprivation can become really angry and feel extremely overwhelmed and anxious, so lack of sleep can be a long-term issue if you regularly suffer from sleep issues.

Ten steps to deal with your anger

If you do have anger issues, it's important to manage them effectively. Here are ten steps to help you deal with your anger:

1. Don't speak out straight away; take a few moments to think. If we speak too soon, we may say things we don't mean and regret. First, take a couple of minutes to think about what you want to say, if you should say it, and how you should say it.

2. Express yourself once you've calmed down. It's best to wait until we're calm before we express anger. That way, you can speak with clarity and authority. Speaking when calm is the best way to get your point across without hurting the people around you.

3. Take a timeout. That's right; timeouts aren't just for kids. Think of them as being a short break during the day that alleviates stress. Sometimes,

taking some time alone can help you get ready for the day ahead. Quiet time can often provide us with a sense of calm.

4. Exercise. Exercise helps with all kinds of problems and issues, including stress and anxiety. With that in mind, it also helps reduce feelings of anger, and it gives you something else to focus on.

5. Problem-solve. Anger is a problem that you need to solve, so if you're feeling angry, identify your triggers and work out possible solutions. Anger itself is not a solution to any problem!

6. Use 'I' statements. Sometimes, a person who is suffering from anger issues tends to blame or criticize others during moments of anger. To avoid this, stick to using 'I' statements to discuss or describe the problem, ensuring you are specific, whilst also being respectful. Saying 'You didn't do [this]' can be seen as a personal attack as it's an accusation. If you say, 'I'm upset that you didn't do [that],' it sounds less attacking, yet it clearly expresses where your anger stemmed from.

7. Use humor to make light of the situation. If you say something funny, it can really lighten up the situation and diffuse any tension. It can also help you face your triggers and increase your awareness as to what is making you angry. However, there's a fine line between humor and sarcasm, and as sarcasm can hurt the feelings of others, it should be avoided as it can cause further tension.

8. Relax! Throughout this book, we've linked regularly to relaxation skills, including meditation. If your anger heightens, you should utilize your relaxation skills, especially deep breathing. Calming music can also help, as can journalling. Taking a short walk can also help you to relax.

9. Don't hold grudges. Grudges actually hold onto anger and other negative feelings, but the power of forgiveness is enlightening. Holding a grudge means you are swallowed up by bitterness, but forgiving others is a learning curve. It can even help you grow and develop in the way you handle situations in the future.

10. Seek help if you need to. Many women ignore the impact of their anger but increasing your awareness and accepting you have a problem is the first

step to dealing with it. Controlling anger is a challenge, and that's why it's important to get help if you need it.

Anger management therapy

We all know what anger is and how it feels because we've all felt it. Anger is healthy and normal unless it escalates, turns into rage, and becomes out of control. Being unpredictable due to anger and your actions can make you feel like you're at the mercy of your own anger, but don't worry; there are many ways you can learn to manage it.

Dealing with anger is complex, as you need to find the strategy that works best for you. Learning to cope with this is the most important thing in the first instance, and you first have to be aware of the problem to prevent yourself from responding on impulse or without thinking.

Many people use things we've covered already to cope with anger. Things like exercise, mindfulness, journalling, or finding something you enjoy doing are great ways to deal with it. You can also try emotional reframing, so you can take your thoughts and put them into a different perspective. As we've mentioned several times throughout this book, perspective is everything.

If you want to want to work on your anger, you need to ensure you should:
- Only target the problems that you need to solve now.
- Focus on the present. In Chapter 5, we talked about focusing on the present, and this type of action is certainly needed when it comes to dealing with anger.
- Monitor your emotions through your mood journal and lean into the CBT techniques covered in Chapter 1.

· Challenge your emotions in your mood journal and work on those
negative thought patterns.

· Try some mindfulness, meditation and breathing exercises to calm
you down. Learning to relax and calm your mind can help you put
things into perspective.

· Personal reflection is a great way to learn to control anger
management issues as it helps you pinpoint the causes. Reflect on
those triggers/causes and consider what you can do to make them
less harmful. Can you challenge them with a positive statement?

Anger management therapy has its limitations. It's all about overcoming your
emotional barriers, as they are preventing you from carrying out your daily life in
a healthy, happy way. Anger can be a problem, and therefore, the therapy itself is
a problem-solving tool. As everyone is triggered by different things, and
everyone's anger differs, the whole process is complex. Always allow yourself time
to work through different strategies to determine which one is most helpful or of
value to you.

Working on anger issues takes time, so there is no quick fix. As a whole, there are
many benefits as it can help you deal with emotions you've been keeping inside, it
can help you to work out what triggers or upsets you and find the root cause, and
it can help you to improve your life and relationships, once the issues are
resolved. Sometimes, group therapy sessions are useful as you get the
opportunity to talk through your issues, meet others with the same problems, and
benefit from the accountability element, which can motivate you.

Remember, when it comes to anger management, the overall aim is to overcome
your anger, and you must want to do that. You often have to work through many
strategies to get to the root of the problem, but they are often only effective if you
want them to work and use them in the right context. Sometimes women are
angry with themselves because of the way they feel about themselves. That's why
in the next chapter, we'll be focusing on you and giving yourself time.

Chapter 9

Time - It's Not Going to Change Overnight

In this chapter, we're going to focus on time because, in order to recover from anxiety, you need to give yourself time. It's not simply your recovery that needs time; it's also you.

Repeat after me... I deserve this time!

Let me fill you in on some facts:

- The CBT methods covered in this book are not a quick fix.
- The CBT methods covered in this book encourage life-long, long-term change.
- Change takes time.
- You deserve time to work on yourself.
- Giving yourself time will help you increase your self-love and self-belief.
- When you feel self-love and self-belief, you can live a happier, healthier life as you feel empowered.
- Your mental health has the opportunity to improve overall due to the shift you feel in mindset.

Why does change take time?

I've been building up to answering this question throughout this book. You'll remember that we talked about changing thoughts, changing reactions and changing habits. However, before we can change, we have to take time to pinpoint them, make an assessment (are they good or bad?), and it's only then that we can work on each of them. We have to create new habits and beliefs to replace the previous ones. Our old habits and beliefs are things we've learned for many years - throughout our lives - and therefore, replacing them takes time.

Some women are frustrated at the prospect that these things take time; however, use this as an opportunity to change the way you view your time by adopting the mantra below:

My time is an investment into my future.

We don't invest money in a business and expect a huge turnover tomorrow, as we accept that this takes time. It's down to you to decide how to invest your time, but devoting it to yourself has many benefits, including:

1. It makes you feel worthy and valued. This may be subconscious at first, but on reflection, you'll realize that you are worthy and you are valuable.

2. It allows you time to care for yourself and get to know yourself. So many women don't tend to their own personal needs and do not know what they really want in life because they spend the majority of their time concerned about others.

3. It allows you to grow and develop, as it's a personal development journey. This leads to long-lasting change, as you're adapting how you think and aiding personal growth over time. This is not just a fad; it's a commitment that turns into a lifestyle.

Everything you've learned so far in this book is taking you on a journey of self-discovery, and this chapter is no different. There's no denying the power of self-belief if you only invest this time in yourself.

As women, we may have been brought up to think that someone who loves themselves is arrogant, selfish, conceited, etc, and that we should put others before ourselves. We can be made to feel guilty by family members if we spend too much time (or money) on our appearance, clothes, make-up, skincare routine etc, and while it wouldn't be wise to spend frivolously, we definitely deserve to treat ourselves from time to time. Self-love is also about much more than material things. It relates to how we speak to and think about ourselves.

At one time, many women shied away from loving themselves for the reasons I have just mentioned, but let's explore why we should all embrace self-love.

Six reasons to embrace self-love

Buddhism is a spiritual religion, and meditation is a key part of its practice. Its teachings are based on four noble truths. They are:

- The truth of suffering
- The truth of the cause of suffering
- The truth of the end of suffering
- The truth of the path that frees us from suffering

The teachings encourage others to look within themselves for the truth in order to seek enlightenment, which incorporates meditation practice. As a result, people who practise Buddhism are in touch with their mind and body. They believe that they can overcome any problems, due to their wisdom, compassion and courage.

While Buddhism is different to CBT, you can see how the belief systems of these two concepts intertwine. As we're talking about self-love here, we should reflect on this famous Buddhist proverb.

"You can search throughout the entire universe for someone more deserving of your love and affection than you are yourself, and that person is not to be found anywhere. You, as much as anybody in the entire universe, deserve your love and affection."

~ Buddha (Quote.cc, 2019)

This quote is applicable to you now, and it's the very reason why you deserve your own love. It's time to focus in on why you should love yourself:

1. It helps you become more effective in your interactions with other people. When we love ourselves and tend to our own individual needs, we are more prepared and able to help others.

2. It builds our confidence. Confidence is so important, and self-love and self-belief are both closely related to this. If you know who you are and recognise your worth, you'll begin to feel more confident in the things you do. Confidence is very different from arrogance, and a self-assured woman is an inspiration to all other women.

3. You no longer need validation from others because you realize that what you say or do, or how you feel, counts. You don't need approval from others either. This builds your resilience, and you take responsibility for your own feelings. This can be incredibly empowering, particularly for women, as we are often raised to look to other people, almost to seek permission and clarification that we are doing the right thing.

4. We feel happy! If we feel self-belief and self-love, we start to embrace happiness, and we enjoy life more and have a more positive outlook. This benefits everyone around us, including our family members and friends. They will all notice these positive changes in you, and you can influence them to be more focused on the good things in life.

5. It leads to an easier life. If you love yourself and feel valued, you're not so hard on yourself. You are able to let things go and don't beat yourself up. That's because you think rationally and can put things into perspective. Chastising yourself for small errors only leads to more anxiety.

6. While this may sound far-fetched, it's true that if you love yourself, you're more equipped to love others. That's because we value ourselves, and valuing yourself and your worth encourages positive relationships with others. Nobody is able to take advantage of you if you truly value yourself.

As you can see, loving yourself has so many benefits, and it influences your personality and mindset too. Self-love and self-belief are superpowers that encourage you to be the best you can be and help others as much as possible. The way we feel about ourselves can also influence our own mental health, including our anxiety. Let's look at this next...

Self-love, anxiety and mental health

There's a clear link between self-love, anxiety and mental health. They often coexist together and generally intertwine. Anxiety can cause mental health and self-love issues, while other mental health issues can cause anxiety to get worse, as well as self-love issues. A lack of self-love can then cause mental health issues, including anxiety. It's a vicious cycle!

In order to review this, we should consider some symptoms of anxiety. As I mentioned in the introduction, some women talk about feeling sick, sweating, an increased heart rate, breathing changes or even numbness or a sense of pins and needles within the body. It's your body warning you that something is wrong.

Anxiety is a mental health issue, but lack of self-love can also cause other mental health issues, such as self-esteem issues, stress, and depression, as well as increasing anxiety issues and panic. Each of these issues encourages us not to feel good about ourselves and they have their own side effects. It's worth remembering that these problems can also lead to sleep issues: another negative element that can impact how we feel.

All mental health issues are complex, but it's important to understand the connection between them and self-love if you want to overcome anxiety or mental health problems. You see, you need sufficient self-love to ensure you value yourself enough to consider your own well-being and happiness. This is especially true if you want to overcome anxiety or other mental health issues. It's an essential aspect of self-esteem and can ensure contentment while improving our greater well-being.

But self-love takes time, and it also takes practice. If you want to develop the way you feel about yourself and improve your mental health, you must practice self-love daily by:

Ø Protecting yourself by ensuring you get rid of the negative people in your life who get a thrill from your pain and loss.

Ø Staying centered and focused on your needs, not your wants.

Ø Forgiving yourself. We have a habit of being particularly hard on ourselves, especially when we're not feeling good. Take responsibility and accept it but try to resolve any issues rather than beating yourself up.

While we talk about loving ourselves, it isn't always easy, and so many women don't know where to start. So next, we'll explore how you can start to love yourself - because you deserve it!

How to start loving yourself in 13 easy steps

Most women want to feel happy, well and fulfilled with their life. They don't want to struggle with anxiety, but often, they can't help it. They don't know where or how to begin. If you want to make positive changes in your life, you should start with yourself, but sometimes there is a stigma surrounding that notion and we feel stricken with guilt for even contemplating the importance of loving ourselves. It's that very thought that is holding you back!

"Falling in love with yourself first doesn't make you vain or selfish – it makes you indestructible."
~ Good Morning Quote (2017)

The quote above is so relatable because it's true. Loving yourself can help you to do better at everything else in your life. It is not a selfish act, but rather an act of self-care that encourages a better, more productive and effective you. It can make a formidable force and, yes, indestructible too.

Love is a powerful tool, but it should certainly start with you. This is why you should always allow time for yourself and work on yourself. Here's how:

1. Never compare yourself to other people. While competitiveness can be motivational, you should compare yourself against your own goals and achievements rather than those of others.

2. Ignore the opinions of others. It's time to accept that it's impossible to please everyone, and why should you be a people-pleaser at the cost of your own happiness? Stop fretting about the judgements of others as they are not always valuable to us. Simply use your own initiative and work towards the things that you want.

3. Learn from mistakes. We all make mistakes, so there's no point in beating yourself up about it. In order to turn a mistake into something positive, learn from it. Ensure that this won't happen again – use the error to instigate change.

4. If you're unhappy with your body, remember this doesn't impact your personal value. The way we look can distract us from achieving our goals, so it's important you don't allow this to happen. Wear what makes you feel confident and happy, but also comfortable.

5. Don't ignore your fears; process them. Perspective is everything, and remember that the things we are afraid of can be overcome. Process your fears by recognising them, use your problem-solving skills to deal with them and then move on.

6. We've mentioned this already in this chapter, but it's important to recognise that toxic people serve no purpose in your life. Sometimes, it's just time to let go!

7. Place your trust in yourself. You are a reliable and dependable woman, and you need to believe that. You need to place the belief in yourself and allow yourself to make good decisions. You know yourself best of all, so there's nobody more capable than you!

8. Don't feel bad about putting yourself first. It's important! As we've talked about in the earlier section, we perform better when we take care of ourselves as we have more energy to dedicate to others.

9. Make sure you take advantage of every opportunity that comes your way. Accept that the timing is not always perfect, especially if the opportunity is a big step for you, but to really get what you desire, seize all opportunities!

10. Be bold! The act of being bold and speaking your mind takes practice, but if you don't do it, you lose the ability to express it. It's like a muscle that needs training, and it demonstrates confidence.

11. Allow yourself to feel everything. While it's good to feel joy and happiness, also allow yourself to lean into the pain when it's needed. If we limit our feelings, it can have detrimental effects on our mental health. We must overcome our feelings of pain, fear, and anger, not suppress them. Sometimes, accepting them and learning to understand them allows us to realize who we are and what we want to change.

12. Be kind! This includes being kind to others and yourself, plus it also incorporates celebrating your own successes. Let's face it; the world is filled with people who love to put another person down. You can break this negative cycle by speaking kindly and ensuring you don't criticize yourself or others.

13. See the beauty in everything. Being grateful is also something that takes practice. Practicing gratitude actually helps you find joy, and it offers you perspective too. The first thing you should do every day is list some things you are grateful for, and throughout the day, notice the other beautiful things around you. Writing it down also helps, as you can reflect on this later in the day.

Do you see how important it is to give time to yourself?

Giving time to ourselves allows us to really focus on implementing change. It's impossible to make so many changes overnight, but that's because self-love is a journey to self-discovery. While evoking change isn't always easy, it is often for the greater good. While not every day will be a walk in the park, we always have the next day to look forward to. This takes us onto the subject of our final fabulous chapter; tomorrow is a new day!

Chapter 10

Yourself - Tomorrow is a New Day

In this chapter, you'll learn how to:

Carpe diem...

> - Because in this chapter, we'll focus on living each day as it comes.

While I'm sure you're familiar with the famous phrase above, we're going to delve deep and explore the reasons why it's important to live just one day at a time, using The VISIBILITY Method.

Even if the day we face isn't easy or enjoyable, or it doesn't go as well as expected, we always have tomorrow to look forward to. Tomorrow can be the day you stay the same, or it can be the day you invent yourself. Whichever you choose, it's important that you act. Make it happen!

What does *carpe diem* mean?

Carpe diem is Latin, and it means 'seize the day.' It is a phrase that was once used in Odes (I.11) by the Roman poet, Horace. Odes was published in 23 BCE, and this phrase has regularly been used throughout the ages. It gives the idea that we should enjoy our lives and live day-by-day, taking each day as it comes.

Carpe diem is basically telling us to:

- Enjoy our lives each day
- Be happy
- Take every opportunity

When it's translated directly, the phrase actually says, 'pluck the day' and suggests that we should live today as if there's no tomorrow. However, while we should remain in the present and not worry or focus too much on the future, it's sometimes a relief to know that we have tomorrow too. The idea of a new day for some people is motivation as it suggests there is an opportunity to start afresh.

How can I *seize the day*?

Of course, it's common to ask this question at this stage, but the truth is you already know. You've been doing it already!

Anxiety issues can be debilitating, but you seized the day when you bought this book and started working through it. It shows that you want to change, and you have the grit needed to seek it out. If you have got this far in the book, you have continued to seize the day because you have made it through 10 chapters, so you have committed time and energy to yourself and dealing with your anxiety. That is a huge achievement in itself, and you should be so proud of yourself.

Everything you've learned so far in this book has led to this moment. In Chapter 1, you had the topic of CBT introduced and considered how it could help you. You've completed activities such as checking in with yourself, keeping a mood journal, and you've identified cognitive distortions. You have also explored ways to overcome negative thinking patterns and change your core beliefs to help you live a more positive life. By doing this, you've already taken action to overcome your fears, as well as any other barriers that stand in your way.

You are a truly amazing and inspirational woman!

While the focus of this book has been linked to anxiety throughout, you've taken back the power by goal setting and following routines and strategies that will lead you to success. You've studied worry and control and assessed how this has impacted your life so you can face your fears while embracing the positives. By now, you realize the importance of self-care and have a clear direction – you understand your needs, wants and beliefs. Being assertive and using strategies that help you concentrate on the present have helped you come to terms with the negativity of the past. You're feeling enlightened and empowered by the decisions you can now make with consistency and clarity.

If you feel like you need to revisit any of the previous chapters at any time, please do so. This book is your best friend. It is here for you, no matter what. It will not rush you or pressure you, so if you feel that you need a bit more time to ensure you have understood everything we have covered together, take however long you need.

Activities such as mindfulness and meditation can play a huge role in keeping the mind calm and helping us figure out what to do next. While it's crucial to concentrate on the now, it's also imperative to have some knowledge of what lies ahead. Everything you have done so far is part of your journey to combat anxiety. While dealing with procrastination can sometimes stop you in your tracks, it's apparent that you're now equipped to deal with that too.

Moving through the maintenance chapter will have demonstrated that CBT is not just a tool; it's a way of life if you want to crush your worrying thoughts and banish your bad habits. Problem-solving is challenging, but throughout your journey, you've displayed resilience and commitment.

Congratulations! You've been seizing the day for a while now, but it's time to take things a step further. You need to keep up the momentum with The VISIBILITY Method so you can continue to keep your anxieties at bay, and stay on your journey to a happy and fulfilling life. Let's recap what The VISIBILITY Method is:

Visualization: - How You Start to Use Cognitive Behavioral Therapy Every Day

Intention: - Turning Your Anxiety Into A Routine

Switch: - How You Pinpoint and Change Harmful Thoughts

Invalidate: - How You Eradicate and Rebuild Your Core Beliefs.

Basic Enlightenment: - How You Stay in the Present

Idling: - How You Move Forward and Just Get Started

Let Go: - How You Really Let Go and Remove Worry and Fear from Your Mind

Instruct :- How You Tell Your Mind to Release the Pent Up Anger Inside You

Time: - It's Not Going to Change Overnight

Yourself: - Tomorrow is a New Day

The VISIBILITY Method is significant here because you are visible – I see you. Many women with anxiety go unseen, and sometimes they even try to stay invisible. After many years of trying to go unnoticed, this can be our comfort zone which is why it sometimes feels easier to stay there. After all, it's comfortable. However, this is a mistake because I recognise your worth. You deserve to be valued, and you deserve to be seen. I've got you, I see you!

It's time to seize EVERY day from now on!

While I believe in you and know you're ready to own your journey, staying present is the most challenging aspect of this book. That's why I wanted to leave you with one more gift. Let's explore some practical ways to stay present:

1. Short meditation practice – I recommend that you start with simply doing just two minutes each day, and then build up from that. You may also benefit from listening to some guided meditation recordings.

2. You don't always have to work alone – having a meditation partner or linking up with a regular group can help you get into the habit of meditating. You can support one another and hold each other accountable.

3. Chimes – mindfulness chimes or bells can remind you to pause, or indicate a specific point during the meditation. For example, chimes may occur at the end of your meditation session to mark the end. You could download an app to chime if you don't have meditation bells or chimes already.

4. Make your intentions known – always set your intentions for the day, first thing, and if you're completing several tasks, set your intentions at the start of each activity. Doing this helps keep you focused and reminds you of what you're doing and why. This allows you to stay mindful of your intention, which helps you maintain your productivity.

5. Take time for reflection – at the end of each day, you should reflect on your day and your progress. You can note down how you practiced being present and anything you find difficult. Think about anything you've achieved and also any barriers you've overcome.

6. Be a teacher – this sounds crazy, right? But this method is extremely useful. If you're feeling upset with someone, frustrated, or stressed out with work, you should imagine yourself as a teacher and observe the learning. What can you learn from this experience and being present? What is causing you difficulty? Is there anything you can't let go of? Or anything you take for granted? This can help you master the art of staying present and improving your techniques.

Anxiety has taken many women to dark places, but when you deal with it, you learn to grow from it. It's part of our lives, and it's much more common than you think. Over time, the stigma surrounding anxiety is reducing. More and more women are admitting that they are anxious while others are educating themselves because they have friends and family members who are suffering. Understanding the issues we've covered in this book is beneficial for you as an anxiety sufferer, but it's also useful for those with a family member or friend who suffers and needs your support.

Assessing your progress

As you arrive at the end of this chapter, it's important to acknowledge how far you've come. I want you to take a moment to assess the impact this book has had on your life.

Ask yourself the following questions:

- Reflect on your thoughts at the start of the book. How have your ideas of CBT changed over the course of reading this book?
- Have you been able to identify and work on some of your cognitive distortions?

· This book leads us to crush our negative beliefs and build new ones. Have you been able to follow the strategies and implement them?

· Can you identify three harmful thoughts and indicate which core belief they are linked to?

· Are you able to goal-set and establish a clear plan of action based on what you need?

· Which three strategies have been the most useful part for you?

· Which chapter was your favorite and why?

· Which chapter did you dislike, and why?

· Is there anything in the book that doesn't work for you, and what do you plan to do about it?

· What's the biggest change in your life to come from this book?

· How will you move forward now? What will you do [what's your plan]?

There are no right or wrong answers to these questions, but they might help you work out your next step, based on what you've learned and what's coming up.

Carpe diem!

"Minutes are worth more than money. Spend them wisely."
~ Murphy, T P. (Khurana, 2019)

Conclusion

In 2013, there were 8.2 million cases of anxiety disorder recorded in the UK (Anxiety UK). This is solely the quantity of documented cases, but there are also thought to be many non-recorded cases too. As I highlighted in the introduction, anxiety is almost twice as prevalent in women than men. Sometimes, women suffer from anxiety issues, and they don't realize what they are battling until it escalates. *Imagine the number of anxiety cases that are unreported!*

One explanation for there being so many cases of anxiety, is because it's much more recognised and talked about than it used to be. Health professionals everywhere are in the know when it comes to anxiety and other mental health issues. There's also widespread knowledge within the general public as there's now so much more education in relation to mental health. There's no doubt that anxiety affects many, many women, and it has a huge impact on so many lives. However, it doesn't have to control you forever. I am proud of you for the steps you have taken so far. You are well on your way to a very different life where your anxiety is controlled by you, rather than the other way around.

Even if you don't suffer from anxiety yourself, but your partner, family member or friends do, you'll have some understanding of just how debilitating it is. There are many levels of anxiety, so what may start off as something small can soon escalate into something more ominous. As many women speak out about anxiety today, many sufferers are not aware that they have anxiety. Sometimes, a woman may be completely shocked by the diagnosis; in fact, they may even question its sincerity. The main focus of this book is to improve the life of female anxiety sufferers by introducing them to Cognitive Behavioral Therapy techniques.

Cognitive Behavioral Therapy is goal-oriented and problem-focused, so it's unlike any other treatments, yet it's highly effective. There are many advantages including it being engaging, holding the patient accountable, and being centered around the idea that our thoughts and emotions impact the way we feel or behave. CBT encourages you to take action to challenge and change the way you feel and behave. It helps people to understand their thoughts and emotions so that they can lead themselves to a positive outcome.

The ultimate aim of this book, from the beginning, was to help you cope with anxiety by focusing on Cognitive Behavioral Therapy techniques, and this has certainly been achieved. While the book focuses on the basics at the beginning, it develops as you go along. This book was deliberately written in a way that allows you to make your journey accompanied by it. It's your guide to enlighten you and improve your life.

I can't promise that it will be a quick process, nor an easy one, but I can promise you that it will be worth it. You are a strong woman and you are becoming more powerful every day. Every choice that you make to challenge your cognitive distortions, every time you tick something off your to-do list because you have planned your time well, each decision you make on the back of well-considered pros and cons, you are becoming a force to be reckoned with. You will inspire other women, your children, family, friends and partner. Trust me - they will support you with this journey, and if there are any people who don't, you may need to consider if you want them in your life. In the same way that we need to eradicate old core beliefs that don't serve us anymore, if people are toxic and hold us back, it may benefit us (and our mental health) to cut them free.

It's likely that this book has already helped you identify harmful thought patterns and destructive beliefs, and then it helps you to overcome these issues. Rebuilding a whole belief system is daunting, and it takes time, so in order for you to succeed, you must be very committed to the cause. This book has also offered you different training, such as improving assertiveness, increasing social skills, and enhancing problem-solving skills. These are all transferable skills that you can use in everyday life, in most work/life situations.

A key takeaway that every woman should gain from this book is that everyone's journey is different, and you can break the cycles of anxiety that impact your life. The VISIBILITY Method is here to guide you through, remind you of your worth and show you that you are not alone in this.

It's important to remember that anxiety can become a serious problem if it escalates, so you should always seek medical advice about your condition. Anxiety and other mental health issues aren't something that we as women should shy away from, as our anxieties are often based on things that we need to overcome.

Another significant takeaway from this book is the importance of perspective. Perspective is how we interpret things using our own point of view, but as everyone interprets things differently, we often see things differently from how others see them. When we take some time to really look at why we think or feel in a particular way, we have the opportunity to explore a different perspective. CBT teaches us those things aren't always what they seem – a bad situation is not always as bad as it initially appears.

So many women suffering from anxiety live limited lives. They make excuses and even sabotage their own healing as they struggle to determine their worth. This book can change the life of someone who feels like the weight of the world is on their back but wants to live their life. It's just about finding what works best for you! While CBT is extremely powerful, don't forget that if your anxiety is severe, you may need to visit your doctor or a healthcare professional.

There are many strategies and activities provided throughout this book, and you should try each of these to see which work best for you. Anxiety is personal to the individual, so your preferred strategies and activities will be different to another woman reading this book. That's because everyone's journey is unique.

Now that you've read through this book and worked through the activities, you have the tools you need to live the life you deserve, free from worry and anxiety. It's down to you to maintain your new lifestyle so that you can lead a happy, healthy life.

You have got the power to make the change!

Nurture yourself by continuing to examine your thoughts, explore your feelings, and challenge your thoughts and core beliefs. Lean into a routine that works for you and set yourself up to win by setting SMART goals. You have the power to grow and develop so you can live the life you desire. Anxiety can force us to shrink and hide our true selves, but you should only ever be you.

It's time for you to take ownership of The VISIBILITY Method. *Are you ready to do that?*

If you want to read more of my books, I've also written about depression and stress. You can check them out here: author profile.

Just for you

A FREE GIFT TO OUR READERS

Get The Top 5 Ways To Help Manage Anxiety - You can start using these top tips right away, which will help you to

control the most aggressive mood swings
and allow you to simply calm down.

Go Here Now To Get Instant Access
https://www.morganknowlespublishing.com/free-book-offer

References

Anxiety UK. *Key Facts and Figures*. Available at:
https://www.anxietyuk.org.uk/wp-content/uploads/2019/08/Key-Facts-and-Figures-2019.pdf (accessed: 08/10/2021)

AnxietyUK. *Key Facts and Figures*. Available at:
https://www.anxietyuk.org.uk/wp-content/uploads/2020/07/Key-Facts-and-Figures-2020.pdf (accessed: 15/10/21)

Aqel, F. (2020) *Trick your brain to stop worrying and overthinking*. Made for minds. Available at: https://www.dw.com/en/trick-your-brain-to-stop-worrying-and-overthinking/a-54483817 (accessed: 19/09/2021)

Babauta, L. 6 Practical Ways to Practice Being Present. Available at:
https://zenhabits.net/presence/ (accessed 07/10/2021)

Bajer, A. (2020) *How to Overcome a Can't-Do Attitude in Your Team*. Available at: https://agabajer.medium.com/how-to-overcome-a-cant-do-attitude-in-you-team-952eef8542ea (accessed: 30/09/2021)

Brainy Quote. *Negative Quotes*. Available at:
https://www.brainyquote.com/topics/negative-quotes (accessed 21/09/2021)

BrainyQuote. *Worry Quotes*. Available at:
https://www.brainyquote.com/topics/worry-quotes (accessed: 27/09/2021)

Brilliant Living. *Six reasons to love yourself*. Available at:
https://www.brilliantlivinghq.com/six-reasons-to-love-yourself/ (accessed: 06/10/2021)

Britannica. *Carpe diem*. Available at: https://www.britannica.com/topic/carpe-diem (accessed 07/10/2021)

Burden, D. (2020) *Having Anxiety is Exhausting – But Time Management Helped Me Manage It*. Available at: https://www.psychreg.org/anxiety-time-management/ (accessed: 18/09/2021)

CalmClinic. *The Reasons Behind Anxiety in Women*. Available at:
https://www.calmclinic.com/anxiety-in-women (accessed: 15/10/21)

CalmDownMind (2019) 3 Powerful Techniques to Stop Worrying (and feel relaxed instantly). Available at: https://www.outofstress.com/stop-constant-obsessive-worrying/#:~:text=%20Why%20Do%20We%20Worry%3F%20%201%20Becaus e,it%20can%20do%20nothing%20about%20a...%20More%20 (accessed 03/10/2021)

Careers in Psychology. *Type of Therapy – Anger Management Therapy.* Available at: https://careersinpsychology.org/anger-management-therapy/ (accessed: 06/10/2021)

Chowdhury, M R. (2021) *What is emotion regulation? +6 Emotional Skills and Strategies.* PositivePsychology.com. Available at: https://positivepsychology.com/emotion-regulation/ (accessed 21/09/2021)

Cognitive Behavioral Therapy Los Angeles. *Anger Management.* Available at: https://cogbtherapy.com/anger-management-los-angeles (accessed: 06/10/2021)

Cognitive Behavioral Therapy Los Angeles. *Assertiveness Training in Individual Therapy.* Available at: https://cogbtherapy.com/assertiveness-training-los-angeles-ca (accessed 21/09/2021)

Cognitive Behavioral Therapy Los Angeles. CBT For Emotion Regulation. Available at: https://cogbtherapy.com/cbt-emotion-regulation (accessed 30/09/2021)

Cognitive Behavioral Therapy Los Angeles. *Cognitive Distortions: All or Nothing Thinking.* Available at: https://cogbtherapy.com/cbt-blog/cognitive-distortions-all-or-nothing-thinking (accessed 03/10/2021)

Cognitive Behavioral Therapy Los Angeles. *Cognitive Restructuring in Southern California Including Los Angeles and Santa Monica* available at: https://cogbtherapy.com/cognitive-restructuring-los-angeles (accessed 21/09/2021)

Cognitive Behavioral Therapy Los Angeles. *Individual Therapy for Social Skills Training in Southern California Including Los Angeles and Santa Monica.*

Available at: https://cogbtherapy.com/social-skills-training-los-angeles (accessed: 28/09/2021)

Cognitive Behavioral Therapy Los Angeles. *Problem-Solving Therapy in Southern California Including Los Angeles and Santa Monica*. Available at: https://cogbtherapy.com/problem-solving-therapy-los-angeles (accessed 03/10/2021)

Cognitive Behavioral Therapy Los Angeles. *Relaxation Training* available at: https://cogbtherapy.com/relaxation-training-los-angeles (accessed 21/09/2021)

Cuncic, A. (2020) *An Overview of Social Skills Training*. Verywellmind. Available at: https://www.verywellmind.com/social-skills-4157216 (accessed: 28/09/2021)

Cuncic, A. (2021) *Negative Thoughts: How to Stop Them*. Available at: https://www.verywellmind.com/how-to-change-negative-thinking-3024843 (accessed: 20/09/2021)

Donvito, Tina. (2021) *101 Anxiety Quotes to Help You Get Through and Lift Your Spirits*. Parade Magazine. https://parade.com/951718/parade/anxiety-quotes/ (Accessed: 07/09/2021)

Edberg, H. (2021) *10 ways to change how you feel*. Available at: https://www.positivityblog.com/10-ways-to-change-how-you-feel/ (accessed 21/09/2021)

Fuller, K. *When Anxiety Turns to Anger: Relationship of Anxiety and Anger*. Discovery Mood & Anxiety Program. Available at: https://discoverymood.com/blog/anxiety-and-anger/ (accessed: 06/10/2021)

Garey, J. *How to change negative thinking patterns*. Child Mind Institute. Available at: https://childmind.org/article/how-to-change-negative-thinking-patterns/ (accessed 20/09/2021)

George, M. (2015) *How to Focus on What You Can Do Rather Than What You Can't*. The Mighty. Available at: https://themighty.com/2015/03/how-to-focus-on-what-you-can-do-rather-than-what-you-cant/ (accessed 20/09/2021)

GetLightHouse. *The Power of Repetition: the secret of successful leaders.*
https://getlighthouse.com/blog/power-of-repetition-successful-leaders/
(accessed: 30/09/2021)

Good Morning Quotes (2017) *52 Inspirational Quotes about Loving Yourself.*
Available at: https://www.goodmorningquote.com/quotes-about-loving-
yourself/#:~:text=%2052%20Inspirational%20Quotes%20about%20Loving%20
Yourself%20,that%20includes%20not%20giving%20up%20on...%20More%20
(accessed 07/10/2021)

Hartney, E. (2020) *10 Cognitive Distortions Identified in CBT.* Verywellmind.
Available at: https://www.verywellmind.com/ten-cognitive-distortions-
identified-in-cbt-22412 (accessed: 17/09/2021)

Healthie. *9 Benefits to Goal Setting for Client Success.* Available at:
https://www.gethealthie.com/blog/9-benefits-to-goal-setting-for-client-success
(accessed: 18/09/2021)

Johnson, D W. (2019) *The Importance of Taking the Perspective of Others.*
Psychology Today. Available at:
https://www.psychologytoday.com/gb/blog/constructive-
controversy/201906/the-importance-taking-the-perspective-others (accessed:
08/10/2021)

Kent.Edu (2017) *Signs of Procrastination.* Available at:
https://literacy.kent.edu/salt_fork/time_priority/timemanagement/procrastinat
ion.html (accessed: 30/09/2021)

Khurana, S. (2019) *Inspiring Quotes to Use When You Want to Say 'Carpe
Diem'.* ThoughtCo. Available at: https://www.thoughtco.com/inspiring-quotes-
carpe-diem-2831933 (accessed 08/10/2021)

Kumar, P. (2018) *21 Beautiful Quotes on Embracing the Present Moment.*
Mission.Org. Available at: https://medium.com/the-mission/21-beautiful-
quotes-on-embracing-the-present-moment-77d7d2e9ecb3 (accessed
21/09/2021)

Lamothe, C. (2019) *11 Ways to Be More Assertive.* Healthline.
https://www.healthline.com/health/how-to-be-more-assertive#start-small
(accessed 21/09/2021)

Lindberg, S. (2018) *Are you Worried or Anxious? Here's how to tell.* Available at: https://www.healthline.com/health/how-worry-anxiety-are-different (accessed: 28/09/2021)

Mackay, H. (2020) *Don't get into a worry habit: It's useless, senseless, worthless.* The Business Journals. Available at: https://www.bizjournals.com/bizjournals/how-to/growth-strategies/2020/03/don-t-get-into-a-worry-habit-it-s-useless.html (accessed: 27/09/2021)

Matthews, S. *Top 10 Ways to Obtain a Can Do Attitude and Find More Success in Life.* Available at: https://thestrive.co/ways-to-value-yourself-and-overcome-cant-do-attitude/ (accessed: 30/09/2021)

Mayo Clinic. (2020) *Anger Management: 10 tips to tame your temper.* Available at: https://www.mayoclinic.org/healthy-lifestyle/adult-health/in-depth/anger-management/art-20045434 (accessed: 06/10/2021)

McLeod, S. (2019) *Cognitive Behavioral Therapy.* Simply Psychology. Available at: https://www.simplypsychology.org/cognitive-therapy.html (accessed: 19/09/2021)

Mind. (2018) *How to Cope with Anger.* Available at: https://www.mind.org.uk/information-support/types-of-mental-health-problems/anger/about-anger/ (accessed: 06/10/2021)

Mind Fit. *Why does it take time to change?* Available at: http://www.mindfitltd.com/faq/why-does-it-take-time-to-change/ (accessed: 07/10/2021)

Mindful.org (2020) *What is Mindfulness?* Available at: https://www.mindful.org/what-is-mindfulness/ (accessed: 28/09/2021)

Mind Tools. *Time Management: Beat Work Overload. Be More Effective. Achieve More.* Available at: https://www.mindtools.com/pages/main/newMN_HTE.htm (accessed: 30/09/2021)

Mind Tools. *SMART Goals*. Available at:
https://www.mindtools.com/pages/article/smart-goals.htm (accessed:
19/09/2021)

Myers, L. *Targeting Success, Develop the Right Business Attitude to be Successful in the Workplace*. Available at:
https://www.goodreads.com/quotes/tag/assumptions (accessed: 18/09/2021)

National Health Services (NHS). (2019) *How it works – Cognitive behavioural therapy (CBT)* https://www.nhs.uk/mental-health/talking-therapies-medicine-treatments/talking-therapies-and-counselling/cognitive-behavioural-therapy-cbt/how-it-works/ (accessed: 17/09/2021)

Newman, S. (2015) *How to be Selfish*. PsychCentral. Available at:
https://psychcentral.com/blog/how-to-be-selfish#1 (accessed 20/09/2021)

NHS. (2018) *Overview – Generalised Anxiety Disorder in Adults*. Available at:
https://www.nhs.uk/mental-health/conditions/generalised-anxiety-disorder/overview/ (accessed 03/10/2021)

NHS Inform. (2021) *Ten Ways to Fight your Fears*. Available at:
https://www.nhsinform.scot/healthy-living/mental-wellbeing/fears-and-phobias/ten-ways-to-fight-your-fears (accessed 03/10/2021)

NHS UK. *Symptoms - Generalised anxiety disorder in adults*. Available at:
https://www.nhs.uk/mental-health/conditions/generalised-anxiety-disorder/symptoms/ (accessed: 15/10/21)

No Panic. *Goal Setting*. Available at: https://nopanic.org.uk/goal-setting/ (accessed: 18/09/2021)

Northpoint. (2020) *7 Tips on How to Stop Intrusive Thoughts*. Available at:
https://www.northpointrecovery.com/blog/7-tips-deal-stop-intrusive-thoughts/ (accessed 03/10/2021)

PsychologyTools. *What is CBT?* Available at:
https://www.psychologytools.com/self-help/what-is-cbt/ (accessed:
18/09/2021)

Quote.cc (2019) *300 Best Buddha Quotes On Love, Life and Happiness*.
Available at: https://www.quote.cc/buddha-
quotes/#:~:text=%20Go%20to%20table%20of%20contents%20%201,free%3B%
20he%20shall%20cease%20to%20be...%20More%20 (accessed: 06/10/2021)

Raypole, C. (2020) *How to Focus on Yourself – and Only Yourself*. Healthline.
Available at: https://www.healthline.com/health/focus-on-yourself (accessed
21/09/2021)

Raypole, C. (2020) *Meet Anticipatory Anxiety, The Reason You Worry About
Things That Haven't Happened Yet*. Healthline. Available at:
https://www.healthline.com/health/anticipatory-anxiety#treatment (accessed:
27/09/2021)

Riopel, L. (2021) *8 Benefits of Cognitive Behavioral Therapy (CBT) According to
Science*. Positive Psychology. Available at:
https://positivepsychology.com/benefits-of-cbt/ (accessed: 08/10/2021)

Robbins, T. *Be Decisive*. Available at:
https://www.tonyrobbins.com/stories/unleash-the-power/be-decisive (accessed
21/09/2021)

Robbins, T. (2018) *Being Present: How it works*. Available at:
https://tonyrobbinsfirewalk.com/being-
present/#:~:text=However%2C%20there%20are%20many%20benefits,live%20
with%20passion%20and%20purpose. (accessed: 28/09/2021)

Rtor.Org (2018) *Why "Love Yourself" Is Good Advice to Follow When Struggling
With Mental Health*. Available at: https://www.rtor.org/2018/04/24/love-
yourself/ (accessed 07/10/2021)

https://www.psychologytoday.com/gb/blog/your-emotional-meter/201711/7-
tips-how-kick-the-habit-indecisiveness (accessed: 27/09/2021)

Schaffner, A K. (2021) *Identifying and Challenging Core Beliefs: 12 Helpful
Worksheets*. PositivePsychology.com. Available at:
https://positivepsychology.com/core-beliefs-worksheets/ (accessed:
22/09/2021)

Schrader, J. (2017) *7 Tips on How to Kick the Habit of Indecisiveness*.
Psychology Today. Available at:

Scott, E. (2021) *Journaling to Cope with Anxiety.* Verywell Mind. Available at: https://www.verywellmind.com/journaling-a-great-tool-for-coping-with-anxiety-3144672 (accessed: 20/09/2021)

Seltzer, L F. (2017) *What's "Emotional Reasoning" -And Why is it Such a Problem?* Psychology Today. Available at: https://www.psychologytoday.com/gb/blog/evolution-the-self/201706/what-s-emotional-reasoning-and-why-is-it-such-problem (accessed: 21/09/2021)

Silva, S. (2021) *9 Ways to Change Negative Thinking by Reframing Cognitive Distortions.* PsychCentral. Available at: https://psychcentral.com/lib/fixing-cognitive-distortions (accessed 19/09/2021)

Smith, M. Segal, R. Segal, J. (2021) *Therapy for Anxiety Disorders.* HelpGuide. Available at: https://www.helpguide.org/articles/anxiety/therapy-for-anxiety-disorders.htm (accessed: 19/09/2021)

Stanborough, R J. (2020) *How to Change Negative Thinking with Cognitive Restructuring* Healthline.com. Available at: https://www.healthline.com/health/cognitive-restructuring#what-it-helps (accessed: 21/09/2021)

Star, K. (2020) *How to Prevent Anxiety from Causing Procrastination.* Available at: https://www.verywellmind.com/procrastination-and-panic-disorder-2584095 (accessed: 29/10/2021)

Star, K. (2020) *Mental Filters and Panic Disorder.* Verywellmind.com. Available at: https://www.verywellmind.com/mental-filters-and-panic-disorder-2584186 (accessed: 21/09/2021)

Stein, M. (2021) *Anxiety and the Art of Doing Nothing.* Psychology Today. Available at: https://www.psychologytoday.com/gb/blog/understanding-the-anxious-mind/202108/anxiety-and-the-art-doing-nothing (accessed: 30/09/2021)

Stewart, A R. (2018) *13 Steps to Achieving Total Self-Love.* Healthline. Available at: https://www.healthline.com/health/13-self-love-habits-every-woman-needs-to-have (accessed 07/10/2021)

Sutton, J. (2021) *Socratic Questioning in Psychology*. PositivePsychology.com. Available at: https://positivepsychology.com/socratic-questioning/ (accessed 22/09/2021)

The Cut. *25 Famous Women on Dealing with Anxiety and Depression*. Available at: https://www.thecut.com/2020/09/25-famous-women-on-dealing-with-anxiety-and-depression.html (accessed 15/10/21)

The Free Dictionary. (1988) "Physical Feelings." Similes Dictionary, 1st Edition, The Gale Group, Inc. Available from: https://www.thefreedictionary.com/Physical+Feelings (accessed: 17/09/2021)

Traister, R. (2018) *Good and Mad: The Revolutionary Power of Women's Anger*. Available at: https://www.psychologytoday.com/gb/blog/nurturing-self-compassion/202002/the-power-and-shame-women-s-anger (accessed 16/10/21)

University of Michigan Health. *Stress Management: Relaxing your mind and body*. Available at: https://www.uofmhealth.org/health-library/uz2209 (accessed 21/09/2021)

Vasisht, P. (2017) *Wants Vs Needs – Understanding Ourselves Better*. Medium.com. Available at: https://medium.com/indian-thoughts/wants-vs-needs-understanding-ourselves-better-96a2c35fbc23 (accessed 20/09/2021)

Wikipedia. (2021) *Aaron T. Beck*. Available at: https://en.wikipedia.org/wiki/Aaron_T._Beck (accessed: 19/09/2021)

www.ingramcontent.com/pod-product-compliance
Lightning Source LLC
Chambersburg PA
CBHW071327140726
47996CB00005B/1861